Blessings of Babel

Contributions to the Sociology of Language

46

Editor
Joshua A. Fishman

Mouton de Gruyter
Berlin · New York · Amsterdam

Blessings of Babel
Bilingualism and Language Planning

Problems and Pleasures

by
Einar Haugen

Mouton de Gruyter
Berlin · New York · Amsterdam 1987

Mouton de Gruyter (formerly Mouton, The Hague)
is a Division of Walter de Gruyter & Co., Berlin.

Library of Congress Cataloging in Publication Data

Haugen, Einar Ingvald, 1906 –
　　Blessings of Babel.

　　(Contributions to the sociology of language ; 46)
　　Bibliography: p.
　　Includes index.
　　1. Bilingualism.　2. Sociolinguistics.　3. Language planning.
I. Title.　II. Series.
P115.H38　1987　404'.2　　87-7882
ISBN 0-89925-226-5 (alk. paper)

CIP-Kurztitelaufnahme der Deutschen Bibliothek

Haugen, Einar:
Blessings of Babel: bilingualism and language planning :
problems and pleasures / by Einar Haugen. – Berlin ; New York ;
Amsterdam : Mouton de Gruyter, 1987.
　　(Contributions to the sociology of language ; 46)
　　ISBN 3-11-011080-6
NE: GT

Printed on acid free paper.

Typesetting: Asian Research Service, Hong Kong. – Printing: Gerike GmbH, Berlin.
Binding: Lüderitz & Bauer Buchgewerbe GmbH, Berlin. Printed in Germany.

To My Favorite Bilingual

Eva Lund Haugen

Preface

Bilingualism is a topic that has been receiving renewed attention in the United States during recent years. The interest has been sparked by the influx of new waves of immigrants from countries that once remained outside the stream of American immigration. In the nineteenth and early twentieth centuries most immigrants were Europeans speaking languages at least remotely related to English. Even the African immigrants, brought in largely as slaves, were in some degree, if forcibly, integrated into the English-speaking population. Those who are now concerned about the latest immigrants are often not aware of the fact that the problem has been with us since the founding of the Republic. They see bilingualism as something new and threatening, not realizing that its problems and pleasures are the familiar experience of millions of their fellow citizens and their immediate ancestors. Americans of English extraction have done their best to suppress information about the linguistic melting pot that has long boiled in our country.

It is the thesis of this book that bilingualism is a long-standing and fascinating aspect of the American experience. Even when it is transitional, as it has mostly been, it can be enriching for its participants. It has furnished shelter and comfort for millions while they gradually became rooted in an American environment. Instead of being looked on as a handicap, we shall here consider it as an asset. That is the meaning of my title, the "Blessings of Babel," as will be explained in the first chapter. Basing myself on the biblical tale that purports to explain the origin of the world's diversity of languages as a curse laid upon men by the Lord, I turn the story around and see the tower of Babel as a symbol of the unity of mankind. It is an ideal — perhaps worth achieving — but having, also, like all human life, its quite considerable problems. I intend to furnish such evidence as I can towards convincing the reader of the preponderance of its blessings.

In doing so I will peek into various corners of the world, beginning with my own experience as a confirmed and intractable bilingual. As one exposed to two languages — and two dialects of each from childhood, I feel I can speak from experience. In a succession of essays, each relating to one aspect of bilingualism, I take up many aspects of the problem. These were not originally conceived as parts of a coherent book, but were written and delivered to various forums as part of a lifetime commitment to the topic. Other essays and books have preceded these, but on closer consideration, I have found that in my more mature years my contributions have circled around certain common topics that called for more attention. So I gathered the essays into reasonable sequences and bundles, suppressing redundancies and giving continuity to the whole.

After introducing the topic in chapter one, I proceed to a brief sketch of my own bilingualism and the general lessons that can be drawn from my experience. I distinguish between a "horizontal" variety, like that of Switzerland, and the "vertical" variety, in which one group dominates another. In chapter three I discuss the various definitions of bilingualism and its actual significance in some countries around the world. I also suggest models to clarify the relationship, and introduce some of the writers on the subject.

From there I go on to discuss concepts that have been introduced to explain the backgrounds of bilingualism, e.g. "ethnicity" in chapter four and "ecology" in chapter five. Here we also make acquaintance with a variety of useful terms, such as "sociolinguistics" and the "sociology of language", "acrolect" and "basilect" etc. Here I also discuss issues relating to a Swedish novelist's use of immigrant language, leading to a Swedish-American farmer's diary and its interesting contents. This brings us to the distinction I make between a "rhetorical norm" and a "communicative norm", which can be illustrated by a vehement quarrel between two Norwegian-American writers.

I also make reference to similar problems in India and in the England of the Normans. These arise as part of a social integration that is the topic of chapter seven, where we discuss the choices that face the immigrant. Shall he/she integrate or remain separate? Most have chosen to do both, all at once. Various examples are given of prominent men who illustrate the problem. This takes us into the world of sociolinguistics, topic of chapter eight, a kind of linguistics that has won not only a name but great prominence in recent years.

From the immigrant group we turn to the problems of whole nations, especially those which face major diversity, e.g. Nigeria. Most nations actually have minority problems that are part of their identity and that inhibit their unity. Chapter nine discusses the problem and leads up to language planning, which is treated in greater detail in chapter ten. Here a model is suggested and refined upon, a perspective that places such terms as "language cultivation" and "purification" into their proper places. In chapter eleven I take up some problems of the implementation of language planning, including the spelling of English *meter/metre*, sexism in language, and the like. The Scandinavian languages beautifully illustrate the fragmentation of a relatively small language area thanks to the language planning of separate but relatively understandable national units. I introduce the term "semicommunication" to describe the situation, which is also known from other parts of the world. At present the greatest influence here is from English, in the direction of "modernization," as suggested in chapter fourteen. In chapter fifteen we concentrate our attention on a little island community that wishes to be a nation, the Faroes, and their language Faroese. From here we turn to the closely related Icelandic, a much larger island community that is in fact a nation, fiercely proud in its isolation and its contact with the rest of the world.

In the next section we turn to closer consideration of Norwegian: forms of address in seventeen, sexism in eighteen (as illustrated for example in Ibsen's dramas), emigrants in chapter nineteen, in relation to their neighbors the Swedes in chapter twenty.

A more general topic is broached in chapter twenty-one, that of Whorf's "linguistic relativity," with some discussion of an American Indian example, which is continued in the next chapter's discussion of bilingual judgments: what is indeed the relation between language and thinking? Finally, we consider in chapter twentythree the reasons offered for language choice. Why do bilinguals choose to use one language rather than another? Bilinguals are seen as persons who make full use of the opportunity offered them of membership in more than one language community.

A complete bibliography of textual references and an index of topics give the reader access to the sources and the contents of the book.

Contents

Chapter 1
Babel

In Genesis there is an intriguing tale that explains the origin of language diversity, well-known as the Tower of Babel story. We are told, as the King James version puts it, that "the whole earth was of one language, and of one speech." But pride filled the hearts of men, and they were misled into trying to build "a city and a tower, whose top may reach unto heaven." The Lord Jehovah found this project to be a presumption, being perhaps concerned that men might usurp His omnipotence, for "now nothing will be restrained from them, which they have imagined to do." In His infinite wisdom He proceeded to "confound their language, that they may not understand one another's speech." They were no longer able to cooperate in the building of their tower, and were "scattered abroad upon the face of all the earth." (Genesis II: 1-9).

Similar stories are known from other cultures. But among the Hebrews the story was associated with the name of Babylon, which, by a false etymology, was understood to derive from a verb *bālal* meaning "to confuse." In the eyes of the predominantly rural and severely religious Hebrews, Babylon, as the capital of the Babylonian and Assyrian empires, was a big and sinful city. The story not only explained why the towers of Babylon had crumbled, but it answered a question that thoughtful men and women must have asked everywhere: why is it that all peoples have languages, but all so different? In the multilingual Near East the natural answer was: the diversity was a curse visited upon men for their sinful pride.

Those of us who love languages, especially if we have devoted our lives to learning or teaching them, find it hard to put ourselves in the right frame of mind to understand the concept of language diversity as a curse. We see in language a source of novel delights and subtle experience, a blessing. But we need only find ourselves in a country, say Hungary, where every sign looks like an abracadabra and speakers shrug their shoulders at our efforts to communicate, to sense some of the terror that underlies the Hebrew view. As linguists we are entitled to offer a basic correction to the Hebrew tale: men were not scattered abroad because they could not understand one another. They diversified their languages because they were scattered. In the story cause and effect have been reversed. When men are separated by barriers of time and distance, their languages deviate in regular, if sometimes astonishing, ways.

The reason is clear, even if the results are unpredictable. As the most distinctive and significant type of human social behavior, language is learned anew by each child in every generation. The child not only can, he *must* learn whatever language is spoken around him. But he never learns it exactly like those from whom he heard it. What we may call his "creative imitation" is not identical with its model, since it is a piece of human craftmanship, not turned out in a factory. The gift of language is no doubt innate and instinctive, but human speech differs, e.g. from the music of birds, by being diverse and relatively idiosyncratic. It is kept from being totally idiosyncratic because communicators are forced to monitor each act of communication by the response of their intelocutors, the ones they are trying to reach. When a group ceases to communicate with another, their speech drifts apart and they develop peculiarities, creating what linguists call "idiolects". As these accumulate, they grow into different dialects, or languages, or language families.

This process has often been obscured by a certain parallel that has been observed between linguistic and biological inheritance. Races and languages have been confounded to the detriment of both, leading to a type of linguistic racism. Linguists, at least scientific linguists, know better, but they are not without fault in having developed a terminology that speaks of "language families" and "mother tongues", the "generation of dialects" and the "descent of words." These are all metaphors that can be drastically misleading, for there is nothing at all in language that is identical with biological descent. *There are no genes in language,* beyond the universal human gift of tongues. When we say that English or German are "descended" from Germanic and Germanic from Indo-European, we are only suggesting that there has been an unbroken transmission of speech habits all the way back to that tribe of Aryan conquerors who issued from the Caucasus or wherever, some five or six thousand years ago, and who succeeded in gradually imposing their language on most of Europe, on much of western Asia, and eventually on the Americas, Australia, and other parts of the world. At every step of the way there were children who learned the language of their elders in their own way, and there were adults who learned or unlearned their languages to meet the demands put upon them by social and political necessity. There are no genes; there is only learning.

That *learning* is the key to every language problem is so obvious as to be almost a truism. Its implications are being worked out in diligent research. We have still to take account of the informal cross-fire of mutual criticism and correction that shapes the process of learning. As children, and even as adults, we have all felt the taunts that were directed at us or our partners when we deviated from the usual norms of speech. Children are often cruel in showering laughter and ridicule on those who speak "differently." As they grow older, they discover differences that stigmatize some degree of social distance. They learn of differences between upper and lower class, the significance of belonging on this or that "side of the tracks," and the speech mannerisms of their peer-group hero. As adults they register automatically, not just that differences exist, but that a speaker is "vulgar," or "stuck-up," or "foreign," and behave toward him on the basis of these identifications. If they lead to antagonisms or prejudice, to the denigration of individuals, or to the exclusion of outsiders, we may feel that these are examples of the curse of Babel.

For the most part we may therefore assume that the gradual drifting apart of dialects and languages is a natural and almost inevitable consequence of the drifting apart of mankind. We cannot be certain, but there is much evidence to support the assumption that all men were once of "one language and of one speech." The fundamental similarities of all known languages almost require some such hypothesis. Insofar as mankind is *one*, and language is man's chief distinction from animals, it is hard to imagine its origin as polygenetic. If we cannot yet find an ultimate point at which the so-called "families" or proto-languages diverged, this is presumably due to the enormous length of time that has elapsed. We may therefore accept the tower of Babel as a profound symbol for man's ultimate unity and for his common descent as a talking animal. The tower is a hypothetical point at which all the converging threads of today's and yesterday's languages meet, and which is best expressed in symbolic terms.

In their efforts to mollify God's curse, people have resorted to various policies. These range from neighorly tolerance to rigid isolation, and from eager acceptance of a new language to brutal suppression of its speakers. Out of this crucible of *language contact* has come a class of speakers who can manage more than one language, the multilinguals or polyglots. To simplify our expression we shall call them all *bilinguals*, defining them as "users of more than one language." This does not necessarily entail a mastery of all its skills or its entire range; it may be enough to understand it when spoken, or to read it when written. In the widest sense even the students in language classes are bilinguals, though one is tempted to call most of them "semi-lingual."

Today there is a vigorous flurry of interest in our country in bilinguals and bilingualism. Some of us would say: about time! The United States has had bilingual problems since its inception, but has always taken it for granted that with time they would go away. The current interest is triggered by many factors: recent Hispano-American immigration, unrest among blacks, sensitivity to minority problems, a touching faith in the power of education to overcome internal discord. Sociologists, educators, and linguists have been mobilized to implement "bilingual programs." These are often

spurred by the congressional Bilingual Education Act of 1968, which recognized for the first time in official American policy that "the use of a
child's mother tongue can have a beneficial effect upon his education."
Linguists have discovered Black English and Chicano Spanish as valid and
highly productive subjects of study. Ethnic groups have been urged to maintain their identity by teaching the native tongue to their children. In communities with a large number of non-English speakers schools with bilingual
programs have been established. Some training in these languages has been
introduced in the early grades in the hope of reducing their sense of alienation in an all-English world. Goals may involve no more than a "transitional
bilingualism," to ease the child's integration into the Anglo community.
There is no deep change in the official policy of Anglo conformity, only
a passing toleration of "linguistic pluralism." Even this is a step forward and
well worth encouraging.

We are hardly unique in the world in having such problems. What is
unique is that in our time a great many populations that speak minority
languages are refusing to accept the status of second-class citizens in the
countries they inhabit. Such refusal was unthinkable so long as most peoples
were locally bound as hewers of wood and drawers of water. Language
problems rarely arose in the Ancient World or the Middle Ages. Only when
governments instituted universal school systems, beginning in the eighteenth
century, did language become an explosive issue. The schools brought into
age-old local communities a force that aimed to homogenize the population,
encasing it in a countrywide mold created by a previously tolerant or indifferent government. The school became an instrument for "mobilizing"
the population, in Karl Deutsch's happy phrase. (Deutsch 1953) The mobil-
ization was to plug the people into a network of communication that would
function fast and efficiently, which would only be possible if one rather
than many languages were spoken. Translation is slow and costly, and interference between codes results in loss of information. The obvious solution
was to insist on one language for each government.

As an illustration we can instance the case of the Swedish province of
Norrbotten, on the Baltic Sea at the border to Finland. Here lives a population of minorities: the Lapps or Sami (as they are now known), whose
status is not unlike that of our Indians, say the Hopi, a people driven back
from their original territory by invaders and assigned to land so infertile
that no one else desires it. (Hansegård 1968: 131). Then there are the Finns,
who like Hispanic speakers in our Southwest, have found themselves on
the wrong side of a border, and are being gradually de-ethnicized, while
they play the role of proletariat in the new nation. (Jaakkola 1971) Finally,
there are the Swedish dialect speakers, roughly like our West Virginia moun-
taineers, who are gradually being forced into urbanization and are discri-

minated against unless they change their speech. Until recently the Swedish school system disregarded all of these varieties (Österberg 1961).

Language is not a problem unless it is used as a basis for discrimination, as it has been used, and especially in modern times. The trend is clearly toward a language shift, a process that not only deprives the minorities of their group identity, but also of their human dignity. The fact that their language is not considered valid in the larger society may make them feel that they are not personally adequate.

What are the solutions? The economic disadvantages of having more than one language in a country (or in the world) are patent and apparently irresistible arguments for assimilation. Groups that refuse to assimilate must be either repatriated or segregated, in the view of many administrators. There are two humanistic solutions that suggest themselves immediately to men of good will: deliberately to inculcate and to promote through education a spirit of understanding of and interest in minority peoples, and to encourage a bilingual policy, so that they are given a sense of being understood by their neighbors.

In principle, this policy is being followed in modern Sweden, according to a law from 1962, which states that the Sami have the right to instruction that is equal to, but not necessarily identical with that which other Swedes get. They are entitled to "an orientation that does not merely communicate knowledge, but also awakens respect for and piety towards the heritage from earlier generations and a feeling of solidarity with their own people." (Ruong 1969) The same spirit has led to a Massachusetts statute that provides for teaching "both in a child's native language and in English." (Kobrick 1972).

The first step in applying our best scientific knowledge to language problems is to become aware that no one's speech is inferior, only different. Neither American Indian nor Samish have been used for atomic science, but their subtleties of expression for their original users are beyond our imagination. Like Finnish in Sweden, Chicano Spanish may be the idiom of a population lost in an alien land, but in its home it is a language of the highest, literary and scientific cultivation. Norbotten Swedish may sound odd in Stockholm, as backwoods or ghetto English does in Boston, but their internal laws permit their users to express anything they need to say. Our problem is how to teach tolerance of difference, and the acceptance of a man or woman for what they are, not for how they talk.

So we are led back to bilingualism, not as the curse, but as the blessing of Babel. Bilinguals have been under a cloud, distrusted by monolingual neighbors, viewed as mentally handicapped by some psychologists. But in many situations in our world, bilingualism offers the only humane and ultimately helpful way of bridging gaps in communication and of alleviating the curse of Babel.

We shall now proceed to examine some of the known characteristics of bilingualism in detail, beginning with my own path to bilingualism. (Haugen 1972b)

Chapter 2

On Growing Up Bilingual

My interest in bilingualism originated as an intensely personal concern. Born as I was in the state of Iowa of Norwegian immigrant parents, my earliest recollections are of the problems I encountered in keeping apart the Norwegian spoken at home by my parents and their friends and the English spoken on the streets by my playmates and at school by my classmates and teachers. The setting was urban and wholly American, with no immediately surrounding neighborhood to support my "foreign" language, contrary to the situation of many rural communities in the Middle West and the Northwest.

Thanks to my parents' adamant insistence on my speaking their native tongue at home, the threshold of the home became the cue to a code switch. As an only child I lacked the potential support of siblings to defy the will of my parents. When coming in from a lively period of play, I blundered many a time in violation of Norwegian idiom. My parents showed considerable tolerance in this respect. My mother, to be sure, being trained as a school teacher in Norway, tried to keep up standards of purity. For the most part, my errors, which I would now call "interferences," were not noted and corrected (Weinreich 1953:1). The Norwegian spoken by my parents in this setting was not only partly dialectal, but had also diverged considerably in the direction of English by adopting English words and phrases in a Norwegianized form.

We never used any other word for a "broom" than the English word, pronounced *brumm* in terms of Norwegian spelling. I recall the amusement and momentary consternation it caused when a visitor from Norway used the Norwegian word *kost* to describe it. We never hesitated to say that we would *krosse striten* instead of *gå over gata* when we intended to cross the street. As travelers we might say *sette sutkeisen på saidvåka* for "putting the suitcase on the sidewalk", instead of *sette kofferten på fortauget,* as our urban contemporaries in Norway would have done. My parents made some efforts to avoid such terms in speaking to well-educated or recent arrivals from Norway. But the words were so common in the usage of the people with whom they associated that they no longer excited any remark, aside from an occasional wry witticism. Historically, the English words were "interferences," or even well-established "loans." In our usage they were part of a new code, a partially merged language, an "interlanguage" if you will, a strictly American Norwegian.

At the age of eight I had the unusual experience of being conveyed by my parents to Oppdal, the rural community in Norway from which they had sprung. (Haugen 1982). In view of the American urban neighborhood where I had lived so far, it was a traumatic experience. My parents were genuinely hopeful that they could "go back home," only to be disillusioned after two and a half years. This period coincided with the first two years of World War I. In this Norwegian interlude I had my first brush with dialect *diglossia.*

Even though I could communicate with the children of neighboring farms, who were my new agemates, my American Norwegian was not adequate. Not only did they use words and forms that I did not know, but they were baffled by my Americanisms. I had to unlearn the interlanguage of my American environment, not just "relexify" it by replacing its English loans with Norwegian terms, but also by adopting a stricter grammatical form of the dialect itself. I recall being bemused by the word for "tickle," pronounced as *kjåttå* /çot:o/ in the dialect, where standard Norwegian had *kile* /çi:lə/.

The pressure for linguistic conformity expressed itself in the usual way, through laughter and the unthinking cruelty of children to one another. They sometimes asked me to talk English, out of curiosity to hear what it sounded like (this was long before English had become a regular subject in the schools). But I refused from sheer fear of ridicule. In those years I hardly used English at all, except perhaps in solitary monologues. On our return it was noticed that I had acquired a perceptible Norwegian accent in my English. So once more I went through the process of overcoming deviations in language and bringing my English back to midwestern standards.

Once these problems were overcome, I had in fact internalized two codes for production: a relatively pure Norwegian dialect, and a relatively pure American dialect. I say "relatively" only because "pure" implies a perfection which I would be far from claiming. Perhaps I should say, "natively acceptable." These two were constantly reinforced by opportunities for use with native speakers. Among my parents' friends, and including particularly my father, I could count on an opportunity to show off my new Norwegian dialect. And of course, my English was quickly reestablished to the level of my agemates in the grammar school.

From my eleventh year forward life proceeded along two rather different tracks: on the one hand home and family, with friends and fellows in the Norwegian Lutheran Church to which we belonged and in which we were active; on the other hand, the American public school and friends I made there, along with such activities as scouting, which I shared with them.

But my parents were now pursuing their goal (especially my mother's) of enabling me to use also standard Norwegian, i.e. the literary language.

Technically, this meant the Dano-Norwegian which has become the modern "Book Language" (*bokmål*) of Norway. (Haugen 1966a) In school I got no support for this endeavor, of course. My mastery of Norwegian was overlooked and if anything discouraged, at least until I got into high school. I can say with assurance that it did not hold me back in acquiring standard written and spoken English. I recall occasional interferences which had to be corrected in my writing, as when I wrote "on Iceland" (Norwegian *på Island*) instead of "in Iceland." In speech there were certain "hard words" that had to be mastered, as when I pronounced "horizon" /hor'izən/ instead of /horai'zən/. But this was no worse than the illiteracies of most of my schoolmates, whose scholastic shortcomings could not be attributed to any "foreign" background. I took to English language and literature, even to grammar, with great avidity thanks to my realization of the linguistic possibilities that my Norwegian experience had implanted in me.

By the time of the generally recognized crucial threshold of puberty, I had in effect acquired six codes: a high and low register of American English, the literate and the vulgate; a local Norwegian dialect in two varieties, the native and the Americanized contact dialect; and an approximation to standard Norwegian: speech and writing. It is hard at this point to say to what extent each of them was productive or receptive. In any case I was clearly conscious of their existence and the problem of keeping them apart.

My reason for recounting this personal background is to illustrate the correlation of one's learning with the social experience of group living. American English grew out of my experience with playmates and teachers in an urban American setting. Dialect Norwegian came from immigrant parents and Norwegian playmates. Standard Norwegian stemmed from my parents and their friends as representatives of the community of cultivated Norwegians in America. In each of these settings I found satisfaction in performing functions that earned me acceptance and praise. Somewhere in this experience lies the key to the worries that many people have about making their children bilingual. No harm can result if the contexts are satisfying and supportive. In that case the problems of integrating two cultures and two languages are not overwhelming to the child. A satisfaction should result which, at least in my case, has never been equaled by the various languages I have learned later in life, mostly in school.

Of course there were problems. How could one be both a Norwegian and an American and identify with both countries? How could one be both a dialect and a standard speaker, identifying with a rural as well as an urban environment? Linguistically and culturally it involved a kind of tight-rope walking, a struggle against interference to achieve the norms of each social group. One remembers mostly the defeats, the lapses that tickled the funny bones of one's listeners. I once tried to explain to some contemporary

Norwegian newcomers the difference between "soft" and "hard" water. I made up the word *hårdvann* for "hard water", which to the unbridled amusement of my listeners coincided in pronunciation with *hårvann* "hair tonic". After World War II, when I was Cultural Officer for the American Embassy in Oslo, I astonished a Norwegian committee by suggesting that a certain person "sit on" the committee *(sitte på)* instead of the correct "sit in" *(sitte i)*. The phrase suggested that he would weigh the committee down with his physical presence. Such problems are part of being bilingual. But the reward of being accepted in two cultures outweighs the problems.

Having put in so much effort at learning these various codes, I was naturally drawn to the profession of language teaching, and on to linguistics, and eventually to a special concentration on bilingualism. (Haugen 1953a, 1956). Many had already written about this problem, especially in Europe, but the delimitation of it as a field of study was novel when I did my research, in the 1940's and 1950's. The problems and the rewards here sketched from my personal biography proved to have been shared by a multitude of people around the world. The problems were not peculiar either to me or to my contemporaries. There has nearly always been a conflict of interest between members of different language communities. Hence bilingualism is ultimately a political and social problem, made manifest in the minds and hearts of the persons who constitute these communities.

In thinking about the problem, it is important to keep the *individual* and the *social* aspects distinct. As we shall see later, one can locate individuals on a two-dimensional chart. On one parameter the various degrees of skill, from zero to native command, and on the other the language distance, from virtual identity to maximum difference. Both dimensions offer interesting themes of definition and research, and they give us some kind of a model to keep in mind.

The pressures exerted by society are of quite a different order. Here it is a question of the power differential between groups. We can think of a situation like that of Switzerland and describe it as "horizontal", a bilingualism without domination by one group over the other. The federalism and the loose-jointed relation of the cantons makes each one a monolingual unit, so that multilingualism becomes a problem only at the official, legislative level. Yet most Swiss speakers are not bilingual, at least not in the languages of their own country. A more explosive situation is the usual one, that we may call "vertical" bilingualism. Here one language group dominates the other in terms of access to power and the benefits that flow from such access. Here we may speak of a *dominant* and a *dominated* group. As social planners we would like to bring the dominant and the dominated together on a plane of equality.

The problem for the community is that of creating an atmosphere favorable to bilingual education both in the dominant and the dominated population. In our Southwest this means the Anglo and the Hispanic communites; in Canada it means the English and the French. Lambert has made the point that "priority for early schooling should be given to the language or languages least likely to be developed otherwise." (Lambert 1974) He has in fact advocated a system of language immersion by the dominant group in the language of the dominated. The situation in our Southwest is just the opposite: the dominated are immersed in the language of the dominant. What we need is immersion programs in Spanish for American children.

To convince those who oppose such programs we need to show them that they are beneficial and in no way harmful to the children. We have to prove that such proposals are not un-American or unpatriotic, and that they make the United States a better place to live. Let us see this as a problem of *social ecology:* keeping alive the variety and fascination of our country, diverting the trend toward steamrollering everything and everyone into a single, flat uniformity.

To put such plans into effect we need more abundant materials at every level of education. Immersion calls for something more than just sampling a language for a few hours a week. Immersion requires living and thinking, even loving and feeling in the new language. It is like learning to swim: as long as one still thinks one will sink, one has not learned to swim. Swimming in a new language requires the provision of opportunity and the ability to communicate successfully with one's own as well the other group.

Now that laws for bilingual education have been passed by Congress and by the legislatures of many states, I can only say that this is an astonishing reversal for one who has experienced the hysteria against non-English teaching after World War I. Now even some ethnic groups that have been weakened with age, like the Germans and the Scandinavians, have awakened to their heritage and are making efforts to keep alive something of what their ancestors brought with them to this country.

What can we hope for as results from bilingual teaching? All depends on giving the dominated, weaker group an education that is equal in value to that of the stronger. In his article on the immersion programs of Canada, Lambert alludes to some of the problems, many of the same I have described above as occurring in my experience. He has noted something he calls an "immersion class French," an interlanguage in which literal calques on English appear, such as *Q'est-ce que c'est pour?* for "What's that for?" We need not take such lapses too seriously. Among other bilinguals such *gaffes* will be understood, even if they sound amusing. They will generally be ironed out when two populations have learned to speak to one another, just as my un-Norwegian or un-English idioms were counteracted by my further social experience. (Haugen 1978, 1980).

Actually, it is the interlanguage of daily life, of the market place, that we want them to learn, not necessarily the languages of Racine or Shakespeare. Test scores are no ultimate proof of the success of a bilingual program. We look for a livelier, more vigorous group life, reduced discrimination, richer experience, and hopefully a more open society than the one we have.

Chapter 3

Bilingual Competence

It is no simple task to define the limits of what we call "bilingualism." There are undeveloped societies, e.g. in New Guinea, where neighboring tribes speak totally different and unrelated languages, but still communicate easily because everyone is brought up to understand his neighbor's language. On the other hand, there is scarcely a single modern nation in which there are not minority groups who are required to learn someone else's language as soon as they leave their birthplace. In nations like Switzerland, Belgium, Finland, India, or Yugoslavia more than one language is officially recognized in the administration of the country.

The problems of bilingualism are of such dimensions that they even appear from time to time in our daily press. We read of Flemish students rioting in Brussels and Louvain against the dominance of the French, while in Canada French students protest the domination of English. In India there is rioting against the imposition of Hindi on the speakers of other languages. The many new nations of Africa are under a necessity of getting along with the language of their former colonial masters, French or English, because their population is split into dozens or even hundreds of languages and dialects. We do not so often hear of the problems in such nations as Greece or Norway, with their dual traditions of writing. The fact is that some degree of bilingualism is now and has always been a part of the experience of most human beings who have not remained rooted to the spot of their birth. It is a social and political problem of some dimensions, and for many it will also be a personal problem.

In this generation the problem has caught the fancy of scholars in several different disciplines. Linguists like the late Uriel Weinreich (1953) and myself (Haugen 1953a, 1956) have concentrated on the problem of keeping separate codes apart. Others have studied the initiation of bilingualism in children; the classical study is by Werner Leopold (1939-1949). Educators like Arsenian (1957) and Macnamara (1966) probed the effect on their schooling. There are important studies from Wales, Ireland, and the United States on this subject. From Europe have come several carefully documented cases of the experience of particular groups and individuals: German children in Estonia (Weiss 1959), a self-report by a German-Italian-English bilingual (Elwert 1960), Latvian children in Sweden (Ruke-Draviņa 1967), an American child in France (Valette 1964), the interaction of Finnish and Samish (Hansegård 1967), of Finnish and German (Wieczerkowski 1963),

Standard and Dialect Swedish (Österberg 1961), Czech and German (Vildomec 1963), to name a few. In the United States and Canada psychologists like Wallace Lambert (1961 etc.) and Susan Ervin-Tripp (1967 etc.) have explored the reactions of bilinguals to various kinds of psychological stimuli, with the object of finding out whether they think differently from monolinguals. Kolers (1968) has explored just how bilinguals store two codes in the mind. Numerous anthropologists have reported on the structure of societies where bilingualism is a part of daily experience, e.g. Diebold (1961), Fishman (1967 etc.), Gumperz (1967 etc.), and Lieberson (1969). From more recent years one may mention Susan Gal (1979) on the experience of Hungarians living in Austria and Nancy Dorian (1981) on Gaelic speakers in eastern Scotland. Political scientists like Deutsch (1953) have provided analyses of the forces involved in language conflict in various countries.

In Canada the tensions between French and English in Quebec led to the appointment of a Royal Commission on Bilingualism and Biculturism in 1963. Its preliminary report appeared in 1965, and the first volume of a voluminous series in 1968. Seminars on bilingualism were held in Canada (Moncton, New Brunswick 1967; see Kelly 1969), Wales (1960), Belgium, and Luxembourg. Under the leadership of Wiliam Mackey an International Centre for Bilingualism was established (Mackey 1965 etc.).

Just what is this bilingualism that is being studied? There are two opposed schools of thought in this matter: those who adopt a *narrow* definition, and those who adopt a *wide* one. The narrow definition may be exemplified in the work of Braun (1937:115): "Active, completely equal mastery of two or more languages." Bloomfield (1933:56) relaxed the requirements by asking only for "native-like control of two or more languages." Let me rephrase these as *native competence in more than one language*. But this is only an ideal, theoretical model: few if any actually achieve this. Most later students have adopted a wide definition, e.g. Hall (1952:14) admitted as a bilingual one who had "at least some knowledge and control of the grammatical structure of the second language." I tried at one time to establish a cut-off "at the point where the speaker can produce complete meaningful utterances in the other language" (Haugen 1953:7). Then Diebold (1961) extended it to include even Indian (Huave) speakers in Mexico who were only passively familiar with Spanish (which he called "incipient bilingualism").

In its strictest interpretation the narrow definition reduces the number of perfect bilinguals to zero. But the wide definition expands it to infinity, since it can include all human beings who have met or associated with speakers of other languages or dialects. This makes its scope so catholic that it is virtually meaningless.

We must find criteria for narrowing the wide definition or for expanding the narrow one until we have a field of genuine interest. We see between *native competence* and *zero competence* a gradient without obvious lines of division from a purely stylistic difference to a dialectal and linguistic one. We can establish arbitrary levels within these two continua. Educators are accustomed to testing students in language proficiency, whether speaking or listening, reading or writing. Linguists are accustomed to describing language varieties, calling some of them styles, others dialects, and still others, languages. Languages are more or less distant from one another, and there is still much doubt about how one can devise a usable scale of language *distance*. But we can set up a theoretical chart to show the complexity of the problem. In two dimensions we are dealing with continua that can only arbitrarily be segmented (Fig. 1):

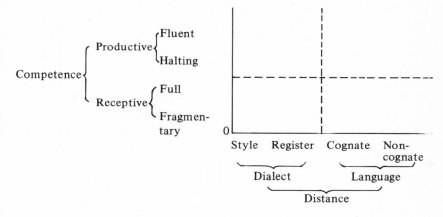

Fig. 1.

One man's dialect is another man's language. Skills are generally proportionate to the needs and compulsion that are exerted on the individual. Many of the same phenomena of switching, interference, and code convergence take place whenever languages or dialects are in contact.

The dimensions of competence and distance each have a breaking point which may be used to bisect the continuum. Competence may be predominantly passive, a characteristic that we will name as *receptive*. Reading competence, often used as a minimum ideal of foreign language learning, is a receptive skill. Children will often listen for months to a language spoken around them before they attempt to use it. Some adults, like the Huave mentioned above, never go beyond reception and are content not to become productive. Production requires the internalization of rules of grammar and social behavior that one is spared if learning only to understand. Even so, the dichotomy is less than clean. Since the speaker can control production, he may even learn to speak without fully understanding all the answers. They may be spoken at a speed beyond his competence. This will certainly be true if he has learned the language by reading only. But in general, production is the higher skill and presupposes a basis of receptive competence.

The breaking point of language distance is that of *mutual intelligibility*. In Germany Bavarian and Saxon are considered dialects, while Dutch is a separate language. Yet there may be less intelligibility between the two dialects than between some varieties of (Low) German and Dutch. Intelligibility is a highly subjective criterion. It may depend on the listener's intelligence, but it may also be obscured by his attitudes to the other language. At the University of Wisconsin students complained that they had trouble understanding two history professors because they sounded foreign: one was an emigré from Russia, the other was a native Texan! Norwegian and Danish are clearly cognate languages, but speakers have learning problems when listening to each other. Children have often not acquired the competence to understand the other, while adults with any breadth of experience have.

The reference above to "attitudes" involves a further dimension that we may call the *functions* of the language. Bilingualism may separate as well as join social groups. Bernard Shaw is reported to have said that the English and the Americans were separated by speaking the same language. Yet their relationship is to some extent what we may call a "horizontal" relation, like that of the cantons in Switzerland. (See Fig. 2)

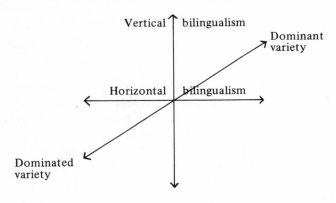

Fig. 2

In most countries where languages abut, there is a marked inequality between the language communities: one is socially, economically, or politically dominated by the other. This is usually the result either of conquest or of migration. In the Americas English and Spanish are dominant not only in relation to the aboriginal Indians whom they conquered, but also to all other European immigrants who settled among them after their rule was securely established. In such cases the functions are gradually shifted from a horizontal to a vertical dimenstion. Mediation goes one way only, from the dominant to the dominated, and the bilinguals are to be found chiefly among the dominated. To put it bluntly: the rulers find it unnecessary to learn the language of their subjects. In Canada 30 per cent of the French speakers know English, but less than 5 per cent of the English speakers know French. The trend is often one of making the entire dominated community bilingual; when that day has come, the original language becomes superfluous and the dominated group may give it up entirely. This is the case of "language death," a term invented by Dorian (1981).

If the dominated group does not give up its language, but continues to use it in daily life, in the home and among friends, the language may acquire a regular function in the community as a mark of informality. If we think of the ideal relationship between groups as being *horizontal*, i.e. of roughly equal status, any tipping of the line will represent inequality. If they are hierarchically arranged, with layers upon one another in an ascending range of power and status, they may even end up in a *vertical* relationship. One idiom may be more or less permanently tagged as appropriate for private or homely discourse, another as approrpiate for public or formal discourse. In a seminal essay by Charles Ferguson (1959) some examples of this were isolated and described under the name of "diglossia." His examples were Arabic, Greek, Swiss German, and Haitian. In each case he saw two closely related language varieties, one playing a role in education and writing, another in speech and daily living. The former he labeled as H for High, the latter as L for Low.

Fishman (1967) adopted the word diglossia also, but extended its meaning to unrelated languages that fulfill a similar function, e.g. Hebrew and Yiddish in the Jewish communities of Eastern Europe, or Spanish and Guaraní in Paraguay. While Fishman's extension is understandable from a purely functional point of view, it leaves the definition open to further widening. E.g., one can say that the learning of written/literary English is a diglossic experience for most children. The same would be true of the learning of Latin or other foreign languages in school. In this sense all educated persons are more or less diglossic.

Let us now reconsider our definition of bilingualism. In the narrow sense it is productive, language-oriented, and horizontal; in the wider sense it may also be receptive, dialect-oriented, and vertical. In practise the narrow definition is more like the popular conception and the more central in our study of bilingualism. The wide definition is interesting as forming either the (inceptive) beginning or the (residual) end of bilingualism. To the narrow definition we may also add the perspective of biculturism, in which ethnicity plays a major role. Only when the bilingual is also bicultural do the problems arise that really challenge the student of language and society. We shall consider this aspect in later sections.

There are terms that appear in the literature of bilingualism for which I have been unable to find any room in my definition. One is the distinction some make between *compound* and *coordinate* bilingualism. Coordinate bilinguals are those who have two clearly distinct systems, compound bilinguals those who have more or less merged them. Elaborate experiments have been devised for testing the distinction in an effort to identify psychological differences in the method of storage. Basing themselves on definitions by Weinreich, psychologists like Osgood, Ervin-Tripp, and Lambert have explored the potentialities of this contrast. (Weinreich 1953: 9-10; Osgood 1954: 139-145; Lambert 1961 etc.). The results have been disappointing; as pointed out by Diller (1967), they reveal chiefly a lack of proficiency, i.e. that the compound bilinguals are simply bad bilinguals. What we really need to explain is the many phenomena that result from *convergence* between codes. The closer codes are, the harder they are to keep apart. Bilinguals are the true architects of convergence.

The pressure to maintain separation is greatest among the users of prestige forms of a standard language. For example, a French-English bilingual who is a writer or a professor will feel a greater urge to keep each of his or her languages "pure". In a relation of dominant/dominated, i.e. vertical bilingualism, the pressure for separation will be greatest in the dominant language. In the everyday give-and-take of ordinary life the pressure will rather be for convergence. As I wrote in my study of Norwegian-American: "His Norwegian approaches his English because both are required to function within the same environments and the same minds." (Haugen 1953a: 72) Gumperz has presented an example from India in which the unrelated Kannada and Marathi are practically calques, i.e. word-for-word translatable. (Gumperz 1967).

Any learning of a language for "tool" purpose should be excluded from the concept of bilingualism. Only if the language becomes a medium for the user's own personality in relation to other members of the community can he be said to enter into a truly bilingual relationship.

The fever of interest that bilingualism has aroused in recent years cannot be treated here. But one should at least mention three works that have a bearing on the theme of this chapter: (1) *Aspects of Bilingualism,* a collection of articles, edited by Michel Paradis (1978), and written by a variety of younger and older scholars; (2) *Tvåspråkighet*, by Tove Skutnabb-Kangas (1981), written in Swedish and now translated into English, a deeply committed statement by a lifelong bilingual (Finnish and Swedish); (3) *Life with Two Languages: An Introduction to Bilingualism* by Francois Grosjean, a psychologist and psycholinguist, who has produced a most attractive textbook, with numerous examples and self-reports by bilinguals. (1982).

Chapter 4

The Ethnic Imperative

> Now the question no longer is how shall we learn English so that we may take part in the social life of America and partake of her benefits. The big question is: how can we preserve the language of our ancestors here, in a foreign environment, and pass on to our descendants the treasures which it contains?
>
> Thrond Bothne, Norwegian-American professor, editor (1898:828)

The meaning of the term *ethnicity* vacillates uncertainly between the two poles of kinship and nationalism, and is a part of the continuum that connects the two. At one end are the ties that hold the family together, whether nuclear or extended, the kind of bond that makes some people go in for extensive genealogical research. At the other end is the ideology that maintains a nation and its culture, to which every citizen is expected to give his loyalty. Ethnicity shares with both a sense of loyalty to one's group, which is larger than kinship but lesser than nationalism. We may call ethnicity an extended kinship and a diluted nationalism.

Ethnicity is therefore a subjective phenomenon, and it cannot be predicted from a person's birthplace, ancestry, or other objective data. The most enthusiastically ethnic Norwegian I have known was a man without a drop of Norwegian blood or background. He is the primus motor and most active member of the Sons of Norway lodge in his Connecticut town. He goes to Norway every summer and makes friends wherever he goes. He knows more about Norwegian literature than most of his lodge mates, and even makes stabs at translating books into English. On the other hand there are all too many immigrants from Norway who have avoided all contact with other Norwegians. They have lost their language, have married Americans and joined American organizations, allowing themselves to be swallowed up in American life, with little if any thought of their homeland and its culture.

These are extreme examples, and most people fall somewhere on the continuum between them. They arrive on these shores with ethnicity intact, a national loyalty. But as the years go by, they gradually move into the new nation, retaining only as much of their ethnicity as does not bring them into open conflict with the new. In the end they are left with little more than the childhood memories of their ancestry, and perhaps sporting a "foreign" name (Isaacs 1975).

What role does language play in relation to ethnicity? First we must clarify just what is meant by the term itself. In a book on ethnicity, Nathan Glazer and Daniel Moynihan pointed out that it was a relatively new word (1975). With the help of the editors of the G. and C. Merriam Company I have been able to trace it just a bit farther back than Glazer and Moynihan. The first use seems to be a pair of articles in the *American Sociological Review* for 1950, where it figures as a synonym for the census term "national origin" (McGuire 1950: 199; Hollingshead 1950: 624).

Launched as a bit of sociological jargon, it has spread to the general public and has taken on a wider sense, thanks to the real life events that have intervened since 1950. A term was needed to describe the loyalty of certain marked groups, above all Blacks and Jews, who could not be covered by the term "national origin," let alone the native American Indians. All of these groups have joined their aspirations for recognition with those that older immigrant groups have long asserted for political and social acceptance (Glazer and Moynihan 1963a).

The topic of ethnicity is of special interest when we speak of the ideological commitment to a particular group. This is certainly the case when the ideology involves active work on behalf of the group and the maintenance of its identity. We must keep in mind that this was true also of the original English settlers of the United States and Canada. They had their ethnicity, which they were able to impose on later comers thanks to their position as first settlers and organizers of government.

We like to think of the United States not just as a new nation, but as a new kind of nation, founded on the eighteenth century ideology laid down in the Declaration of Independence. This involved a commitment to the protection of "life, liberty, and the pursuit of happiness." But when it came to organizing social life and the institutions that would govern the nation, the identity imposed was English. Non-English-speaking immigrants had to yield to this ethnic language if they were to be accepted at all. English ethnicity had little use for anything that was not white, Anglo-Saxon, and protestant (WASP).

The term "ethnicity" has therefore come to be a "minority" nationalism, in the sense of politically dominated. An "ethnic encyclopedia" planned for the United States included all manner of immigrants from Europe and Asia, not to speak of Africa; it also included American Indians, religious groups like the Mennonites, and linguistic groups like the Basques, which lack a homeland of their own. But the English are missing.

When I wrote my major study of the *Norwegian Language in America* (1953a), the term had not yet become popular. But I devoted two chapters to the struggle of many Norwegians to maintain their language in their churches, schools, communities, and homes. When the first boatload arrived, in 1825, it was taken for granted that they would soon be absorbed into the American nation. As their numbers grew, and they succeeded in establishing large and solid communities in the Midwest and Canada, but also in such cities as Brooklyn, Chicago, Minneapolis, and Seattle, they created a Little Norway in which their language and their ethnicity could flourish for a hundred years.

Their churches were almost wholly Norwegian-speaking down to World War I (1914). Higher schools like Luther College in Decorah, Iowa, used Norwegian as the language of instruction well into the twentieth century. Societies and lodges of all kinds were conducted in Norwegian. Newspapers, as the cement that bound them together, flouished in the years down to mid-century.

Popularly the ethnic community was known as *Det norske Amerika* (The Norwegian America), or by more romantic souls as *Vesterheimen* (The Western Home), in imitation of the Icelandic Vestur-Ísland (West Iceland) about the Icelandic communities in America. In this ethnic world *Norskdom* (Norwegianness) was cultivated as a unifying force that also set the members off from their fellow citizens of other ethnic origins.

Most of its members were also busy learning English, as they worked in an American or Canadian community. They pridefully participated in the novel political and commercial system, which gave them freedom and often even prosperity. Toward the beginning of the century, in my boyhood, *Det norske Amerika* was fully alive and enjoying its greatest flowering. My parents initiated me into it, conferring on me that dual ethnicity discussed above, which I have enjoyed ever since.

This world lasted from the founding of Norwegian churches and newspapers in the 1840's and well into our century. Norwegian services came to a virtual end in the 1950's. The major newspapers died along with their subscribers: *Minneapolis Tidende* in 1935, *Skandinaven* in Chicago in 1941, *Decorah-Posten* in Decorah, Iowa, in 1972. Down to 1924 the community was fed by new immigration, at the same time as it was depleted by the loss of many younger members, especially in urban areas.

The change-over from Norwegian to English did not occur without conflict, often between generations. Many a battle was fought on the floor of church meetings and in the bosom of the family between the immigrant generation and their offspring. In rural communities the transition was more gradual, for here the pre-World War I contact with American life could be quite minimal. In the cities life was more open, since Norwegians seldom isolated themselves in ghettolike areas, and did not meet color lines in moving out of the poorer sections as their prosperity grew.

The loss of the mother tongue in home and church could be a bitter experience. It is well known that a second language learned in later life often fails to convey the cultural, emotional, or religous power of the first language, the mother tongue. Even with my entire schooling in English, my Norwegian background somehow makes a Norwegian poem or quotation warmer and more deeply moving than its English equivalent.

In working out my *Norwegian Language in America* (1953a), I resorted (among other sources) to the United States census. However inadequate, it confirmed my expectation that Norwegians were slightly more retentive of their language than the Swedes and a good deal more than the Danes. The much better Canadian statistic of 1931 made it possible to include also the Icelanders. While only 14.2% of the Icelanders had lost their Icelandic utterly, twice as many Danes or 29% had lost their Danish. Of the Swedes 23.7% had lost their Swedish, while 24.9% of the Norwegians had lost Norwegian — not a great difference. One can assume that the Danes were more urbanized than the Swedes and the Norwegians, while the Icelanders have a special loyalty to their language. This kind of study has been extended to other ethnic groups, especially by Joshua Fishman in his classic book *Language Loyalty in the United States* (1966a). He went on to show in detail how ethnic loyalty is associated with language loyalty.

In the typical bilingual community, however, it is often not a question of a black and white confrontation between the languages. When languages are in contact, they tend to develop in parallel directions and even to merge. For Icelandic this has been treated by Haraldur Bessason (1967, 1971) and much earlier by the illustrious explorer Vilhjalmur Stefansson (Stefansson 1903). Speakers who maintain the ethnic language will inevitably, often unconsciously, make concessions to English. It will be quite normal for a dialect-speaking Norwegian to say: *Koltan jompa over fense ut i fila* (The *colts jumped* over the *fence* out into the *field*) where a corresponding farmer in Norway would say: *Folan hoppa over gjerde ut i åkeren.* The grammar is exactly the same, but the significant words have been replaced by English. Words like "colt," "jump,", "fence'. and "field'. have become a part of his everyday vocabulary, pronounced and inflected in Norwegian (*colt* is masculine, *fence* is neuter, *field* is feminine).

Whatever rhetorical purists may think of this development, it is no more peculiar than the fact that English distinguishes between the Anglo-Saxon *calf* and the French *veal,* which is the calf when it is butchered and cooked. The American immigrant dialect served the ethnic community admirably. It brought them a step nearer to the new culture and its language, forming a kind of bridge to save them from plunging into icy waters. The language serves as a valuable shelter for ethnic development. Before they realize it, their thinking has moved word by word out of their ancestral world into the new one. They have shaped a new instrument out of the old tongue.

Before I began working on the problem, very little had been written. But I found in the literature available so many parallels to my experience of the Norwegian-American development that I decided to collect all the studies I could find. This became my book on *Bilingualism in the Americas* (1956, continued in 1973a). Throughout the Americas one could identify similar developments. Wherever one language was politically and socially dominant, e.g. Spanish and Portuguese in Latin America or English in the United States and Canada, other ethnic groups, including Indians, Blacks, Eskimos, and other Europeans tended to accept the majority language. Even if they did not at the same time abandon their own, they began speaking it in a way that suited the new culture of their country. This was true even of the French speakers in Canada. Among the Norwegians even cultured speakers could fall into bilingual traps. The great writer O.E. Rölvaag had to have his manuscripts checked when they were to be published in Norway.

We are inevitably led to the conclusion that it is very difficult to maintain an ethnic language in the shadow of another, dominant language. One recourse is to practice a degree of social segregation, as do for example the Mennonites. Here language is a powerful supportive factor in keeping the elect apart from the worldly. For one thing, it precludes intermarriage by supporting endogamy. Otherwise it means a special effort on the part of parents in creating a native-speaking environment in the home, the school, or the church, or best of all, by immersing their children in the old homeland for a time.

Whatever the problems, the experience is not a mental handicap. It is an extension of experience, a window into another world, and an aid in keeping alive a sense of identity with the past and their kin.

In 1953 I dedicated my book to my parents, "who first introduced me to the pleasures and problems of bilingualism." My personal experience has been that the pleasures far outweigh the problems. But the very fact that bilingualism in our dynamic society appears to be generally unstable and evanescent suggests that many have found that the problems outweighed the pleasures. Many adults have sadly expressed regret at not having learned their parents' language. To them I can only answer: That was either because you resisted when they tried, or because they mistakenly thought that the learning of their language would be a handicap.

There is no doubt that many have considered bilingualism a handicap, especially since the witch hunt of 1918. Intelligence tests seemed to prove that Mexican Americans were handicapped, overlooking that their economic status often kept them from having adequate access to English. During World War II it appeared that foreign languages were in short supply, leading to an emphasis on learning them. New waves of immigration have encouraged the setting up of bilingual schools. It is doubtful that these will promote language retention by minority groups. But it may contribute to giving some ethnic speakers a new pride in their own identity, which will make them better citizens of a pluralistic America.

Chapter 5

An Ecological Model

It has long been a passion on my part to see language in relation to its human environment, for which I adopted the term "ecology of language" in 1971. Among those who helped inspire this view was Kenneth Pike, according to whose "unified theory of the structure of human behavior," language and society are seen as sharing "many kinds of characteristics." (Pike 1967: 641) In his chapter on "the context of behavior" he observes that a society, like a language, may have unity and variation at the same time. There may be subgroupings and interlocking groups "where various individuals are simultaneously members of different groups with different functions" (Ibid.: 643). While such views are the essence of sociolinguistics, I have found it fruitful to adopt the widely used term "ecology" and to apply it to the variation of language.

In recent years linguists have increasingly concentrated themselves about the uniformity of language in a monodialectal community. In such a world speakers agree substantially in phonology, grammar, vocabulary, and any other feature of language. Deviations are a matter of individual performance, following a famous distinction between *langue* and *parole* launched by the French linguist Saussure. This line has been pursued by Noam Chomsky and his followers, who have largely rejected *parole* in favor of "a completely homogeneous speech-community" (Chomsky 1965: 3). This is of course a purely theoretical community, hardly a real one (not even found at M. I. T.). One can imagine an approach to it in a tightly knit elite or professional group, or perhaps an isolated tribal community, though I have only hearsay evidence for this statement. To me it is more congenial to replace this homogeneous model with a heterogeneous one, developed out of the cooperation of linguists with social scientists. The model is an old one, growing from the discipline known as *dialectology*, and now usually comprised under the term *sociolinguistics* (among linguists) or *sociology of language* (among sociologists). I cut the gordian knot by calling it *language ecology*.

An important attempt to correlate social structures with linguistic repertoires was made by John Gumperz in an article entitled "Types of Linguistic Communities." (Gumperz 1962) It is tempting to develop the ideas there presented into a model representing my personal observations and including also the kind of styles observed by Labov (1972) and going all the way to the use of wholly unrelated languages as studied by Fishman (1971).

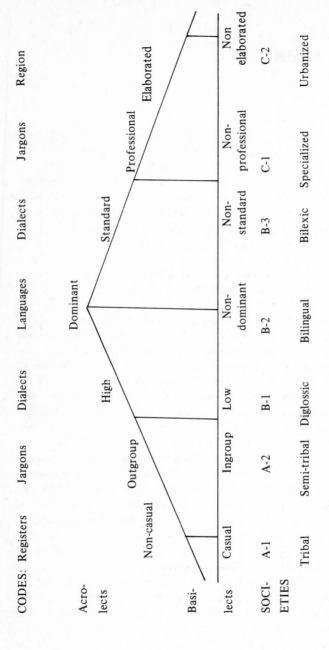

Fig. 1: Codes with Societies

We may begin with the acquisition of a child's first language, the normal, casual language of its immediate environment, the family and the playmates. If we take this as the base line for all later language learning, we may call it the child's *basilect* (a term from Wm. Stewart 1964). This may of course be multiple, but at the moment we are interested only in its contrast, the *acrolect*, a variety that is imposed on the learner from above, either by school, by older peer-groups, or by adults.

At the level of the basilect all languages are equal: there is no difference between societies. But by the time the child has attained his acrolect, a complexity has been imposed that corresponds to the complexity of society itself. Gumperz sees a division into three types: the *tribal*, which is at the hunting and gathering stage; the *intermediate*, with a complex system of social castes and classes; and the *urbanized*, in which class distinctions have changed into professional specializations combined with a less stratified, more democratic organization. We may call these, respectively, societies A, B, and C, and represent them graphically in two ways: either as Fig. 1: "Codes with societies," as lines reflecting language distance, or Fig. 2: "Societies with codes," societies split in various ways: the former reflects the linguist's view, the latter the sociologist's.

Even in A-1, the simplest of societies, as in the Great American Basin, anthropological linguists like Voegelin have shown that there may be differences between what he calls *casual* and *non-casual* registers. The latter often uses antiquated words and forms in special ceremonies preserved by the medicine men (Voegelin 1960). In what may be called *semi-tribal* life (A-2), there is a learning of trade languages for dealing with out-groups, as in the case of Swahili in East Africa.

In the stratified B-societies we can distinguish at least three types: B-1, with a *High* style used for special purposes, such a formal lectures, church rituals, or legal documents, roughly what Ferguson (1959) has called *diglossia*. With Ferguson we assume a considerable language distance, but still within the same language, in what we have called the wide definition of bilingualism. In B-2 there are states that represent the narrow definition, which we may regard as true bilingualism. An example may be England after the Norman invasion, where the acrolect was different and mutually incomprehensible to speakers of the basilect, i.e. Norman French vs. Anglo-Saxon. Here the social relation is one of dominant vs. dominated.

In B-3 the distance is reduced to a point where we can speak of two dialects, one standardized and the other oral. One former dialect has been promoted at the expense of the others. So the Francian dialect of the Île-de-France advanced to become French, leaving Norman and Gascon as dialects, or even, with the disappearance of their writing traditions, as mere patois (in the French conception). If a name is needed for this situation, one can

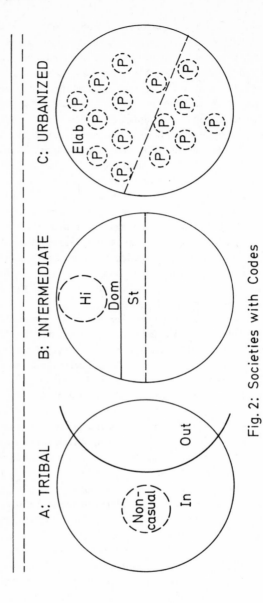

Fig. 2: Societies with Codes

call it *bilexia* in reference to speaking of two *lects,* one dominant and the other dominated.

If we now consider the C-societies, we meet a situation that develops out of B into one where the mass of the people is for the first time given the schooling that makes it literate in the standard. In societies like the American, where social stratification is fluid, and upward as well as sideward mobility is great, the trend will be toward distinctions based on professional training and specializations. Jargons arise for disciplines like medicine, for crafts like automobile repairing, for specialties like linguistics, in which members will recognize each other by their respective jargons. The final state (C-2) suggests a distinction based largely on education: elaborated vs. non-elaborated (Bernstein 1962).

Such either-or categorizations raise questions that have been widely discussed. A problem that is relevant here is whether such societies can be described as having *norms.* The fact that two languages/dialects exist within the same society means that the norm is under constant pressure, so that it loses much of its stability. We must probably assume not only *interference,* i.e. the overlapping of two codes, but also *code switching,* the use of two codes successively, and finally *borrowing,* i.e. the incorporation of novel elements into the norm.

The tape recorder has made it possible to fix informal speech and to analyze it as we might the texts of written languages. The development of sociolinguistic theory, above all by William Labov (1970 etc.) has made it possible to handle what was once called "free variation" and find its social correlates. Even so, the possibilities for individual and creative variation go well beyond any present theory. We can only use experience and common sense (now often called "intuition") to guide us in our understanding. The ease with which natural bilinguals may reshape the norms of their respective languages is still unexplored and may require a radical revision in our thinking.

A stimulus to such rethinking can be found in the writings of various students of Scandinavian immigrant language in America by Folke Hedblom (1975 etc.), Nils Hasselmo (1974), Sture Ureland (1975), Iver Kjaer and M. Baumann Larsen (1973, 1974). One may also look to studies of Estonian by Els Oksaar (1979) and of Hispano-American by Donald Lance (1969), Douglas Shaffer (1975), and Guadalupe Valdes-Fallís (1976). I have been privileged to study some of the American-Swedish material in the Uppsala archives of the Swedish Dialect and Folklore Institute.

Immigrant society is highly dynamic. Immigrants who are not dispersed tend to cluster with fellow countrymen. In the rural Midwest, long the goal of many Scandinavian immigrants, they formed settlements clustering around a Lutheran church, where their own language was preached and taught. Here they could maintain their language and learn only as much English as they needed for economic and political contacts. But their children and children's children were exposed to the English-language school and an ever more mobile society. As long ago as 1950 I set up a model for the transitional ecology of such communities. Speakers with full command of the immigrant language were designated as A, and masters of English were B. Intermediate speakers, i.e. bilinguals, were either A-dominant (Ab), balanced (AB), or B-dominant (aB). The differences constitute a continuum: we may find modified A-speakers (A') or B-speakers (B'). In an immigrant community the trend will historically be from A to B, but as long as there are speakers still using A, all the varieties can be found in synchronic togetherness (Haugen 1953a: 370).

In my field work I was most interested in second-generation bilinguals, who shifted codes readily and had no great hesitation about introducing loanwords from English. Although they might be somewhat deficient in both languages, they were remarkably consistent. They were proud of their bilingualism and often showed normative feelings by commenting on their own inadequacies. They sometimes remarked unfavorably on persons who adopted an excessive number of English words *(engelsksprengt)*, while those who tried to speak a pure Norwegian were felt to be "stuck-up."

Certain views which I advanced on this topic some years ago have been under discussion more recently. In 1960 I was visiting Sweden. I had just been reading the last volume of Vilhelm Moberg's tetralogy about Swedish emigration and settlement in Minnesota (Moberg 1956). These novels have since been translated into English, and they were condensed into two magnificent films, titled *The Emigrants* and *Unto a Good Land.* These were widely seen and highly praised in this country. What can not appear either in the English translations or the films is Moberg's idiosyncratic use of American-Swedish dialog in the volumes that deal with the settlement in Chisago County, north of Minneapolis, in the 1850's.

While in Sweden, I read a critique of Moberg's use of English words by a Swedish scholar (Mjöberg 1960). He objected on aesthetic grounds, basing himself on what we may call a Swedish rhetorical norm. My own impression was rather a number of cases where Moberg seemed to me to depart from realism, the more peculiar in view of Moberg's self-proclaimed realism. The result was that I published an article in the Swedish press, perhaps rashly attacking his American Swedish as "unrealistic and improbable." It reminded me of the many deliberately concocted humorous samples. The article stirred up a hornet's nest and provoked Moberg (who was then still very much alive) into angry replies in defense of his practice. He cited the many letters and diaries he had read, written by American Swedes. He referred above all to the diary of one Andrew Peterson, a farmer in Minnesota.

Peterson had kept a diary from 1854 to his death in the 1890's. He gleefully pointed out that this diary, unknown to me at the time, was available at the Minnesota Historical Society.

On my return to Wisconsin I made a special pilgrimage to St. Paul to study the Peterson diary. My suspicions were verified: Peterson wrote as one might expect. A number of Moberg's examples were due to misreading of his handwriting, possibly by inattentive librarians. Only one of the words to which I had objected proved to be confirmed. Peterson did indeed use a word that Moberg adopted for frequent use: *speak meeting.* This expression, unfamiliar to me as English, and not listed in any American dictionary, appears to have been peculiar to the Baptist sect to which Peterson belonged. They seem to have called what I would describe as "testimonial meetings" by this very special word. It is, accordingly, a legitimate word, though more limited in its appropriateness than the usual *miting* from "meeting."

One of my criticisms of Moberg concerned the fact that he had made no use of the only scholarly study made of the Swedish of Chisago County. This was by Professor Walter Johnson of the University of Washington, a native of the community who was thoroughly familiar with its dialect (Johnson 1942). Moberg brushed aside the criticism, alleging that he had no use for scholarship, having made his own observations (but not in the community). In a later article Johnson pointed out that the study of diaries and letters is a poor substitute for listening to the living speech of the present-day community. (Johnson 1971) He supported my contention, writing that the speech of the pioneers "was not a hodgepodge, an indiscriminate mixing of American and *småländska* phonetic and structural patterns." He showed in some detail how many of Moberg's anglicisms were not part of general usage in the community.

Among the principles that I saw as entering into the bilingual norm was the fact that form words are seldom borrowed, e.g. "how" or "as" (cf. Moberg's *how många* for "how many", *as du forstår* for "as you understand"). (Moberg 1956: 32-34) Also that close cognates are often replaced by native equivalents (cf. Moberg's *Och nu vi go* for "And now we go.") Compounds are usually either borrowed as units or retained (cf. Moberg's *statekörkan* and *svenskmakad* for "state church" and "Swedish made"). (Moberg 1956: 53)

One can apply to Moberg the remarks by the very able Swedish-American writer Ernst Skarstedt, written in 1914. He said that only two writers of fiction had succeeded in "writing American Swedish absolutely correctly, i.e. get in just those English words with just those distortions that are really used by the common man." He criticised writers who had created sentences like *Jag tror inte, hon regretted it* ("I don't think she regretted it") or *Om vi inte råkas nu här on earth* ("If we don't meet now here on earth"). (Hasselmo 1974: 101).

Hasselmo developed a theory of borrowing called "ordered selection." (Hasselmo 1974) He granted that in principle any English word could be borrowed. But in performance there are five levels of choice: whole words as the most likely, then derivative suffixes, then morphological suffixes, then form words, and finally, prosody. Thus a speaker who wishes to say "the tough guys" may decide to use a Swedish plural: *de tough-a guy-ar-na,* or an English plural: *de tough-a guy-s-en.* But he is not likely to say *the tough-a guys.* In studying Swedish speech in Moberg's own community, he found a high degree of elasticity in the borrowed lexicon, but not complete chaos.

We may call this elastic norm a *communicative* norm, and we shall look more closely at it in the next chapter.

Chapter 6

The Communicative Norm

In reference to language the idea of "norm" is both ambiguous and slippery. It may refer to a standardized language like French, codified in grammars and sanctified by an Academy, taught in schools, and written by authors — but spoken by no one, except under duress. Deviations from such a norm are deemed to reveal one's lack of a proper education, and if it is unintentional, is regarded as a barbarism. If it is intentional, it may be acceptable as a stylistic variation, either as a mockery of the "lower classes" or as a relaxation of standards, a kind of "old shoe." I have earlier called this a *rhetorical norm,* since it has been the ideal of rhetoricians and their grammatical henchmen for lo these many centuries. Scientific linguists have often rejected it, at least in theory, and have proclaimed that it is their task to *describe* linguistic norms and not to *prescribe* them (Haugen 1966b: 51).

In bilingual communities there are nearly always educated writers who express scorn for the deviations of daily speech from the rhetorical norms of their language. An interesting example can be drawn from a journalistic dispute in the Norwegian-American group in the year 1881.

Two rival editors of Norwegian-language newspapers in Minneapolis fell into a rather vitriolic discussion about language. They were both university-trained men of well-known urban families, immigrants from Norway within the decade, still in their thirties, and editing secular weeklies for their countrymen. One of them was Professor Sven Oftedal (1844-1911), a clergyman, who edited *Folkebladet* ("The People's Paper"). The other was Luth Jæger (1851-1925), editor of *Budstikken* ("The Messenger"). Jæger was anticlerical, so they had other things than language to feud about. But over some months of the year 1881 this was their topic.

Interestingly, the anticlerical editor was the one who upheld the rhetorical norm. He severely castigated his clerical rival for "bad" Norwegian. He was especially critical of his practice of interlarding his Norwegian with English terms, more or less assimilated. Oftedal replied that he wrote as he did in order to be understood by his readers. To this Jæger retorted that as a pastor and a professor of theology he had a responsibility to the growing generations to give them models of the "best possible Norwegian." As an editor he was also a teacher, "with the duty of maintaining the mother tongue and thereby also the desire to remain in touch with what is going on at home in the fatherland." With a touch of irony he continued that "it would be a different matter if Professor Oftedal could not help mixing and mistreating the language, as he so often does in his paper, but his position as a professor forbids our believing that. . . . So it must be because he either does not wish to bother translating various English words and terms into Norwegian, does not have the time, does not want to, or thinks it is impressive to ornament his paper with these borrowed feathers, in order to show that he knows a little more than his catechism, as the expression goes. We cannot know, of course, what the professor's real motivation is, but it must be one of these or all of them together." (*Budstikken,* Feb. 8, 1881)

If we consider his collection of incriminating examples, however, we are likely to find, as I did, that many if not all of the English terms are such as do not easily lend themselves to translation. They include words and expressions highly characteristic of American political and economic life, such as "deadline," "pay as you go," "dark horse," "figures do not lie," "drawbacks," "a perjured villain," "common sense," "party vote," "logrolling," and "filibustering." These are difficult to handle in any language except as loanwords. In the good pastor's text they are variously treated as integrated loans, or more often as switches, shown by being set off by Roman type in an otherwise Gothic text or by quotation marks. Some of the abusive terms quoted from American politicians he has left in English, he writes, "for decency's sake."

His critic maintained that he could easily have replaced them by Norwegian words. But it is clear that our theologian had the feeling that most of his readers had learned about these things since immigration and would therefore understand them best if one used the precise English words instead of some approximate equivalent in the mother tongue. He did so, of course, in full awareness of the patchwork result and the violation it constituted of the homeland rhetorical norm. That he still did it is especially interesting, since pastors were usually norm models for the standard language among the immigrants.

We need go no further into this particular historical incident. It illustrates my main theme, the question of how and whether one can speak of a norm in a bilingual community. For every immigrant group one can document endlessly the often futile and partly misguided attempts to maintain the rhetorical norm of the homelands. The ability to maintain any norms whatever of one's mother tongue in an environment where one nearly always hears and reads another requires continual vigilance, a vigilance I have described as "linguistic backbone."

It also requires that one keep in constant touch with home base, i.e., that one have a chance to test one's competence against the developing and ever-changing norms of the homeland. For immigrants this would have required either frequent travel to Norway, laborious and expensive in the age of steamships, or extensive reading of its current literature, for which only a few had the taste or inclination. At the very least it required that the speaker be in touch with a large body of monolinguals among his countrymen, who would normally be exposed to the same influences as he.

Situations like these compel us to abandon the concept of a rhetorical norm in favor of one that may be called a *communicative* norm. This takes into account the special situation of the bilingual speaker (or writer). It is more like a spectrum, embracing the wide variation of situations in which a bilingual finds himself. Our Norwegian cleric implicitly acknowleged the fact that his readers were also familiar with English, though perhaps imperfectly, since they still preferred to read their news in Norwegian. He was therefore in all likelihood closer to his readers than our more academic editor.

The communicative norm with which I am most familiar is one that assumes a relatively, if not absolutely, stable bilingual community. Such are less common among American immigrants than in some other parts of the world. Our country has promoted a rapid tempo of assimilation through the public school, and through the relatively mild segregation that immigrant groups have been permitted to maintain. One need only turn to India to find communities where different linguistic groups have been in contact for centuries without assimilating or giving up their distinct languages. A significant factor has here been the caste system, which prevented crossing over through exogamy and personal friendships.

Nadkarni (1975) reports on a dialect of the Konkani language as spoken in the Indian state of Karnataki. This is an Indo-Aryan language spoken by a relatively small, but self-important group living among a population of Kannada-speaking Dravidians. Though they are fluent in Kannada, the Konkani refuse to accept it as their own. But clearly without knowing it, they have adopted the relative clause structure of Dravidian. Their Konkani has become a *contact dialect* by incorporating features from other dialects or languages. In a similar way the English spoken during the Norman-French domination of England no doubt grew to be a contact dialect of Anglo-Saxon, a Franco-English that it might be appropriate, in modern jargon, to call "Franglish."

Those who cling categorically to the rhetorical norm either deride or deplore contact dialects and will flatly deny that there is any norm whatever in their usage. Like our normative editor, they hold that such infringements on the rhetorical norm are due, either to laziness, moral deficiency, or ignorance, i.e. an intellectual defect, or to snobbery, a social defect. A visitor from Norway undertook to criticize Midwestern American speakers: "Strictly speaking, it is no language whatever, but a gruesome mixture of Norwegian and English, and often one does not know whether to take it humorously or seriously" (cit. Haugen 1953a: 57). Nils Hasselmo, in his volume on American Swedish (1974), provides us with a rich flora of similar comments by Swedish observers of their countrymen in the period of active immigration. A favorite word to describe their language was "rotvälska", a term used in Sweden about a creolized gypsy language. In English we might substitute the word "mishmash."

But Hasselmo also found Swedish commentators who recognized the need and justification for a wider spectrum of usage in an American bilingual community (Hasselmo 1974: 86). To this I can add the judgment of a Norwegian-American pastor (not the one cited above), who wrote in his memoirs that "mixing was not done to be affected, but came so naturally that one simply does not notice it. Even we pastors and others who might regard ourselves as 'cultured' often fall into this sin of 'mixing'." He added, "When one lives among these people and learns to understand the circumstances under which they live, one will forgive them." (S. Sondresen, cit. Haugen 1953a: 58)

There is something familiar, perhaps even universal, about this situation and this conflict of views. On the one hand are those who either in the name of the cultural "Great Tradition" (as Fishman has called it) or in defense of language uniformity condemn any deviation from the rhetorical norm as a barbarous deviation. On the other hand are those who defend deviation or cultural differences in language as rooted in specific circumstances of communication, a relativistic rather than a normative or absolutist view.

When Labov (1969) defends the "logic of non-standard English," he is taking the same position vis-à-vis a deviant variety of English as did the Swedish-American writer G. N. Malm when he asserted and defended the existence and validity of a "Swedish-American" language. In 1919 he advocated its use in literature and demonstrated by his own writings how "important it is, in describing Swedish-American types, to permit them in their dialogs to use their own, uncorrupted, often unjustly ridiculed everyday language" (Malm 1919, cit. Hasselmo 1974: 91). One may look similarly at Black English, a contact dialect with substratum elements of African. Like the speaking of immigrant dialects, it gains one no power in the general community, being associated with low-status groups. Once we recognize that much of what passes as humor is a screen for antagonism and unjust discrimination, we will sympathize not only with the anti-defamation league of the B'nai B'rith, but also with the American Polish League that is trying to stop the thoughtless use of Polish jokes.

Criticism of Hasselmo's (and by implication my) views of the bilingual norm was offered by Ureland, who did field work among residual speakers of Swedish in Texas (Ureland 1971 etc.) In a review he rejected Hasselmo's theoretical model of "ordered selection," discussed above: "To the present writer such normative statements regarding the acceptability or grammaticality of certain structures should not be the task of a bilingual study. The sociolinguistic situation of American Swedish is not of such a nature that it allows for categorical rule statements" (Ureland 1975: 10).

A somewhat similar critique was offered by two Danish scholars, Iver Kjær and M. Baumann Larsen (1973, 1974). There is especially one text with forms that are so extraordinary that it serves as a paradigm example. This is part of a conversation by a Danish woman aged 82, who had not been back to Denmark since she emigrated at the age of 28. When the interviewer asked her if she had taught her son Danish, she replied: "Ja, *he* kan tale det, and *he* forstår alt, hvad jeg siger. And *even my* datter-*law, she* er *born* engelsk, *you know,* men *she* sitter og *listener* til os, så sagde: ja I kan ikke tale om mig *anyhow,* for jeg kan *guesse* mig til, hvad det er, I siger." (Yes, he can speak it, and he understands everything I say. And even my daughter-in-law, she is born English, you know, but she sits listening to us, then said: well, you can't speak about me anyhow, for I can guess what it is you're saying.)

The most conspicuous feature of this text is the introduction of the pronouns *he, she,* and *my.* The use of discourse markers like *you know* and *anyhow* is common enough, since they are not as closely tied to the structure. One is struck by her use of *and* and the rather uncommon loanwords *guess* and *listen,* to be sure imbedded in Danish constructions. Throughout the whole text she quite unselfconsciously shifts from language to language. One can hardly be surprised that her daughter-in-law understood her "Danish."

Only one of my 250 informants came close to this kind of mixture, and she was also a person who emigrated in her maturity into an immigrant community. They have failed to establish adequate separation of the languages. Perhaps one should class them as a new category, in my old classification as *ab* or "disadvantaged learners." Hansegård has suggested "semilingual" *(halvspråkig)* for such persons (1968). But they are such only in relation to the outside world: in their bilingual environment their two "half languages" add up to a whole. Like our Danish woman they may say *I* levede or *I will never care* for at have så *much land* ("I lived", "I will never care to have so much land") (Kjær/Baumann-Larsen 1974: 425).

If one is to make a theory out of these examples, it would be that they have not disproved the hypothesis of bilingual norms, but that by their conspicuous deviation they have confirmed it. If we conceive of bilingual competence as a set of co-occurrence rules, it may simply be that the bonds of co-occurrence have been weakened by constant exposure to conflicting norms. If the features have been psychologically "tagged" for one or the other language, we may suggest that for such speakers the tags have fallen off. The situation is reminiscent of some developments in pidgin languages, but our informant has not created a true pidgin. She picks an uneasy path, wavering from one language to the other, uncertain of which to select. Such informants are precious, though this one unfortunately is beyond our reach. One would wish to know more of her life and mentality.

As far back as 1970 Nemser made me aware of what he called "approximative norms" (Nemser 1969). In 1972 I granted that "in the world of the bilingual anything is possible, from virtually complete separation of the two codes to their virtual coalescence." (Haugen 1972) But in any given community a norm grows up which we may well describe as a bilingual communicative norm.

Chapter 7

Social Integration

Under the label of "bilingual education" the problems of immigrant and minority speakers have become matters of some concern. Many Americans have felt a certain alienation with their country. Ethnic identification has persisted in spite of the loss of ethnic languages. Resistance to the leveling trends of American life has emerged.

Studies have therefore been initiated by agencies of the United States and Canadian governments tackling the very problems that have long been thought insignificant. Injustices, segregation, and discrimination are topics of national inquiry. Laws for bilingual education have been passed and are being implemented with varying success, chiefly aimed at Blacks, Chicanos, Puerto Ricans, and Indians. (Andersson and Boyer 1970; Saville and Troike 1971; Paulston 1974; Fishman 1974b) While these are labeled "bilingual programs," they are much more than that. They are attempts to right wrongs that may be basically social, but that manifest themselves as language barriers and learning problems.

Will in fact the knowledge patiently accumulated by scholars be brought to bear on these practical problems? Or has once again a huge boondoggling project been initiated without direction, a new pork barrel for the benefit of a few? Without trying to solve these questions, I can only point to the need for answering them. We may recall that France has never taken a linguistic census, in spite of the fact that there are large and persistent communities where such native languages are spoken as Basque, Breton, Alsatian, and Provençal, the last a kind of French that deserves to be considered a separate language. In asking just how language functions as a socially integrating or disintegrating factor in America, we are also asking just how it feels to speak Welsh in England, Sorbian in Germany, Frisian in the Netherlands, Greenlandic in Denmark, or Samish in the rest of Scandinavia. We are even referring to the meaning of being a Gastarbeiter in Switzerland or Germany, for that is just what most immigrants were in the Americas.

In referring to immigrants here, I am using the term synonymously with "minority group member." Much has been written on minority group theory. What used to be called "the marginal man" has now come to be "the ethnic," reflecting a new attitude. "The foreigner in our midst," once perceived as a vague threat to American institutions, has come to be seen as an enrichment of American life, a man or woman with an "ethnic heritage." (Fishman 1965b)

On his entry into a new society the immigrant is faced with three successive choices.

(1) He or she must decide whether to learn the language of the new society. if (as we assume) it is different from his own. We may call it the problem of language *acquisition,* now the fashionable term for language learning in a natural situation.

(2) He or she must decide whether the old, native language is to be maintained. This is the problem of language *maintenance,* which brings up many questions: how, on which occasions, and for how long?

(3) The third choice grows out of the second: if he or she chooses to maintain it, how will it be used in practice? Will he keep it separate from the first, or will he switch back and forth and possibly let one of them "contaminate" the other? We may call this the problem of language *separation.* Here we may also discuss questions of switching and borrowing and the development of the language under these conditions.

Each of these choices has what Dell Hymes has called "social meaning" in his "ethnography of speaking." (Hymes 1962). A positive answer to questions of acquisition, maintenance, and separation gives us an entirely different profile of social adaptation and integration than does one that is predominantly negative.

The problem of language acquisition is fittingly introduced by the words of a Norwegian immigrant of a century ago. One Syver Holland (from the farm of Håland) composed a ballad entitled *Wisconsinvisa* ("the Wisconsin ballad"), which won a certain popularity among the immigrants (Haugen 1949). It gives a both humorous and poignant expression to the bafflement of the average immigrant:

Jau – i Fyrsten dæ gjek lit paa skakka,
Daa me landa paa framande Jor,
Av dæ Maalet, som folket her snakka,
Skjyna me 'kje eit einaste Ord.

Læra Spraaket va nokot, som leitte,
Ofte stod me mæ skamfulle Fjæs:
Naar ein Yankee deg sporde, ka du heitte,
Raakte jamt, at du svara honom: Yæs!

(Well – in the start we were certainly troubled,
As we stepped on this far-away strand;
Of the language that people here babbled
Not one word could we understand.

Learning English was a struggle and strain,
Many times we just stood there, red in the face:
When a Yankee would ask for your name,
All you could answer was often just "Yas!")

The ballad, of which I include only two of its many stanzas, reflects the view of the average uneducated, but not illiterate immigrant, who felt himself to be handicapped by his initial language deficiency. Even so we must recognize that he brought with him all the varieties of expression pertaining to his social status and educational background in the homeland. There were religious differences living comfortably within the Lutheran state church that erupted in America into fierce factional battles and resulted in the formation of numerous warring church bodies. We may compare with Fishman's observation that Hungarian immigrants from the time of the Russian invasion, mostly young students and intellectuals, found little to identify with among the older Hungarian emigrants with agricultural and laboring background. (Fishman 1966b)

Among the Norwegian immigrants there grew up an active American-inspired Sons of Norway organization, but it was too secular for the taste of many church people: they played cards, danced, and were even reputed to indulge in alcohol! Among the rural immigrants, on the other hand, there arose a so-called *bygdelag* movement, a kind of old-home organization for social get-togethers. (Lovoll 1975). But even among these there were differences: some fiddled and danced (e.g. those from Telemark and Setesdal), while others prayed for their souls (e.g. those from Stavanger and Rogaland).

Individuals reacted differently. An enlightening example was Peder Anderson (1810-1874), who emigrated from Bergen in 1830. He settled in Massachusetts, where his sister, who had married an American, was already living. (E.L. Haugen and I. Semmingsen 1973; E.L. Haugen 1974) He was a gifted young man with a good schooling, and he found work as a bookkeeper in Lowell's growing wool industry. He married an American woman and rose to affluence. He early devoted himself to intense work on the English language and showed a vivid interest in American life and institutions. But he also maintained a close epistolary contact with his relatives back home and even helped some of them to emigrate. He twice returned to Bergen and did much to increase understanding between the two countries. There is no evidence that he used Norwegian in America.

In later years he wrote a short autobiography while on a visit to Norway. Although he could still write Norwegian, his style shows interesting errors in syntax, though no borrowings of English vocabulary. He often turns the order of words around, e.g. *I begyndelsen dette var langsomt* (In the beginning this was lonesome) where Norwegian requires the order *var dette*.

An even more notable example is the author Hjalmar Hjorth Boyesen, who emigrated at the age of 21 in 1869 (d. 1895). Although he started out in the Middle West, his ambition was to become a writer. To do this he left for Boston and took lessons from an elocutionist to get rid of his Norwegian accent. He wrote his first novel *Gunnar* (1874) in English and succeeded in getting it published through contacts he made in the Harvard Library (e.g. the ballad scholar Francis Child and William Dean Howells, editor of the *Atlantic Monthly*). His successful début led him on to the literary world of New York and a professorship at Columbia. He looked with some distaste on his hard-working countrymen in the Middle West, married an American woman and became a guru of the literary scene. But the themes of his most successful books, whether fictional or critical, remained Norwegian. It was as a purveyor of romantic literary themes from Norway that he made his mark. (Glasrud 1963).

A third example might be Thorstein Veblen, born in a Norwegian-speaking community in Wisconsin. Typically, he did not go to St. Olaf College, where Norwegian was strong, but to its non-Norwegian and non-Lutheran rival across the river, Carleton College. He did make some use of his Norwegian background by translating the Old Norse/Icelandic *Laxdale Saga* into American English, though with the ulterior purpose of demonstrating a historical parallel to the boss rule of American cities. But his claim to fame consists of works not only written in English, but a particularly abstruse English. One of his critics has attributed his doctrines of "conspicuous waste" and of the "leisure class" to his Norwegian origin, but it was also an American pioneer view, equally attributable to Thoreau. (Dorfman 1934)

For those immigrants who settled among their peers and fellow ethnics *maintenance* was no problem. Most immigrants shied away from personal isolation and the giving up of their national identity. In most instances the very decision to emigrate was what could be called a "network" decision. They sought the support of kin or friends, coming (like the first boatload of 1825) in groups drawn together by the hope or promise of a common fate. Early comers could offer later ones tickets or employment. These factors led to the rise of a mother-tongue minority group in the new land.

Minority groups have been intensively studied by recent social scientists, e.g. R. A. Schermerhorn (1964). He called his model of minority-majority group relations a case of "power group theory." The group encounter causes a configuration of power relations that functions as an independent variable. Incorporation, or assimilation, depends on the orientation of the respective populations. The dominant group may show traits of racism, social distance, or active prejudice, and it may also be eager to assimilate the weaker group. But this group may be militant or segregative, or it may be eager to be assimilated. If the dominant group restricts access by denying the "social rewards", the dominated group may adopt "forms of closure", at least in the first stages of confrontation (Schermerhorn 1964: 246).

Such study reinforces the obvious: that immigrant society is one in which the immigrant can function most easily. Here in his own churches, societies, occasions, and daily encounters he can use his own language as he wishes, in ways that are not controlled either by homeland standards or by "foreigners." It is like an old shoe, comfortable if not always beautiful. To establish his membership it is not necessary even to speak the native tongue all the time, or in any particular way, so long as he is understood and his speech is acceptable to those for whom it is intended.

The first function of immigrant society is to postpone the immigrant's assimilation by a process of gradual acculturation. (Teske and Nelson 1974). The difference is that acculturation does not require an immediate change of values or of reference group or of individual psychology. Assimilation is a one-way street, but acculturation gives the immigrant a new home instead of making him homeless. The Norwegian author and pastor Kristofer Janson wrote in his memoirs from America that in the Minnesota of 1880 he would have been startled in the Norwegian settlements if he had met a man who did not address him on the road in Norwegian. English was in fact a dead language. (Janson 1913, cit. Haugen 1953a: 39). Teachers had to threaten children with punishment to get them to speak English in the schoolyard.

As we have seen above (Chap. 6), there could be considerable variation in the degree of confusion of languages that became normal in such bilingual communities, depending on such factors as *age, education, language talent,* and *motivation.*

Writers with an inclination to humor or satire have often been known to lampoon the language of their countrymen for its deviations from the rhetorical norm. An American Finn from Michigan purports to write in what he calls "Finglish." Two samples show that he is really representing English in Finnish pronunciation: *Las senssi kerit kas* ("Last chance get-it gas"); *Iits kai kaaru pauning or ket paunit* ("Each guy got to pounding or get pounded"). (F. Karttunen and K. Moore 1974).

An American named James Kirk produced a book of "Scandinavian dialect verses" entitled *The Norsk Nightingale* (Kirk 1905, 17. ed. 1929!) One sample will do: "Dar ban a little faller,/ Ay tenk his name ban Yim,/ And nearly every morning / Ay used to seeing him." While I have never heard a Scandinavian use "ban" for all forms of the verb *to be,* the poem does illustrate some typical problems: *d* or *t* for *th, y* for *j,* confusion of *a* and *e,* etc.

An important aspect of the bilingual's function is the *switching* from one language to the other. Michael Clyne has specially investigated the switching of Germans in Australia (Clyne 1967, 1972 etc.). This is evidence of the bilingual's dual mastery and reflects his complete social integration into the new society. The switches normally take place at breaks in the sentence pattern, and the speaker displays his confidence that the listener is with him. Acquisition, maintenance, and separation are all demonstrated.

Only in recent years, through the rise of a new discipline called sociolinguistics, has it become respectable for a scholar to pay attention to such curious phenomena. We shall take a closer look at this discipline in the next chapter.

Chapter 8

Sociolinguistics: A Challenge

Since bilingualism involves an interaction of language and society, it has come to be included under the umbrella of *sociolinguistics,* now recognized as a new interdisciplinary field. The term aligns it as a kind of linguistics, so that some scholars prefer to call it *sociology of language,* which makes it a part of sociology. This term is probably a rendition of the German *Sprachsoziologie,* which has long been established in Germany. In America the term "Sociology of Language" was used as long ago as 1953 (Hertzler 1965), and in France there was a "Sociologie du langage" (Cohen 1956). The term Sociolinguistics first appeared as a heading in the international *Linguistic Bibliography* in 1967.

The word appears to have been coined by Haver C. Currie, then a teacher of English at Houston University in Texas (Currie 1952). It was first launched among American linguists by William Bright (and A. K. Ramanujan) in 1962 (Bright and Ramanujan 1964). Bright also organized the first conference on the topic in 1964 (Bright 1966). Among those participating was Charles A. Ferguson, then director of the Center for Applied Linguistics in Washington, D. C. The flood of writings that followed these occasions is too voluminous to report on here. It is no coincidence that 1964 also saw the launching of Noam Chomsky's theoretical reorientation of linguistics at the summer Linguistio Institute (Chomsky 1965). The ensuing split in linguistic interests was profound and enduring.

Among the many issues that one can suggest as of interest in sociolinguistics I shall discuss the following: (1) What is the focus of sociolinguistics? (2) What are its units? (3) How can sociologists and linguists cooperate? (4) How can societies be characterized for their language use? (5) What meanings can we attach to the distinction between bilingualism and diglossia? (6) How can one identify and perhaps predict a language shift? (7) What roles do conscious attitudes and overt language planning play in such shifts? (8) What are the uses of sociolinguistics?

(1) As the *focus* of sociolinguistics Wm. Bright has claimed that "linguistic diversity is precisely the subject matter of sociolinguistics." (Bright 1966: 11) Specifically, he would limit it to "the systematic covariance of linguistic structure and social structure." To this I would add the minimal diversity, a relative uniformity, within a small and tightly knit community. In the effortless communication of an in-group there is social pressure for uni-

formity. Beyond this there is the partial understanding which I have called "semicommunication" (e.g. within Scandinavian, cf. Haugen 1966c) and a range that includes the total incomprehension of unrelated languages.

Diversity and uniformity are therefore not exclusive, only complementary aspects of the major problem of sociolinguistics: the formation of language norms in the hot crucible of social interaction. Norms are not necessarily either homogeneous or consciously formulated, but do involve such relatively uniform minimal codes as we may call *sociolects*. A sociolect and its formation is identifiable as the central focus of sociolinguistics. It is an abstract of the sames in the idiolects, or personal norms, including only those features that mark a speaker as belonging to a given speech community.

(2) The *units* that distinguish one sociolect from another are much like those isoglosses that dialectologists have long employed. In America we often identify Australians by their pronunciation of the diphthong /ey/ as /ay/. An Australian who in Boston tried to buy a *spade* was met by a baffled sales clerk until she pointed one out for him. Having had a similar experience with *pail,* she reported to a friend: "You Americans talk funny: you say a 'pile and a shovel' when you mean a 'bucket and a spide.' " In a Norwegian rural dialect that I have studied, Old Norse *ganga* 'go' is apocopated and circumflected to /gàng/; but one family conspicuously has reduced the same form to /gang/. So a single isogloss can distinguish anything from a continent to a family. Presumably, the larger the group and the greater the language distance, the greater the number of such isoglosses.

The special problem of sociolinguistics involves also taking into account class, not just regional dialects. As noted above, these may be vertical, involving power differentials. In this field William Labov's studies of Martha's Vineyard and the lower East Side of New York have already become classics. (Labov 1965, 1966). His methodology has been widely emulated. By limiting himself to a small number of phonological isoglosses or criteria, he succeeded in showing a high statistical covariation between the criteria and the major socio-economic levels, the lower, working, lower middle, and upper middle classes. While these are not precisely "classes" in the Marxian or old European sense, we need not quibble about the word. But one may very well ask whether one can really speak of four different sociolects here. I suspect that we have a basic New York City sociolect or even dialect, what Stewart has called a "basilect," which children learn and many adults retain as their informal language.

But those who by accident of birth or by educational achievement have succeeded in escaping from the "lower" and "working" classes, have acquired an ever more active command of the prestigious "acrolect," which is at least a passive part of the language competence of most New Yorkers. The ability to use it on being asked to perform such formal tasks as reading aloud or even reading lists of words is a function of one's upward mobility.

(3) The solidity of Labov's results are in part due to the fact that he could build on a Columbia University sociological study of New York's lower East Side. From a population of 100,000 this study had pinpointed a sampling pool of 988 individuals who were identified for their social status. Labov could then select with confidence from this pool. My own experience in doing field work on Norwegian-Americans in the Middle West included being challenged by a sociological friend. He found my methods too informal. But his methods involved a technique which I had neither the resources nor the know-how to perform. I went around the community and asked my way until I found those who would and could talk to me. It has taken computers and tape recorders, not to speak of foundation grants, to reach Labov's level.

As one trained in the more informal methods of dialectology I can see another major difference. By reducing the number of his criteria, he ends up with very little general information about the sociolects he is studying. He has sacrificed depth for the sake of breadth of coverage. Even if one could teach his lower-class informants to pronounce his five criteria in the upper-class way, they would still sound lower-class. Grammar, syntax, and word choice would still be a dead give-away. The dialectologist may require interviews that last for hours, or even days and months, to probe deeply into the informant's dialect. We cannot exclude either method from the arsenal of sociolinguistics. The wide-ranging identification of socially relevant criteria needs to be supplemented by the burrowing exposure of the individual's total communicative competence, from sound to sense.

(4) In their effort to find ways of characterizing whole societies for their *ways of speaking*, sociolinguists have made various suggestions. Hymes has called for an "ethnography of speaking", a study of the speech activity of a community as a system that varies cross-culturally and may include a multiplicity of codes within one community. (Hymes 1962) Gumperz has suggested "verbal repertoire" as a cover term for "the totality of linguistic forms regularly employed in the course of socially significant interaction" (Gumperz 1964: 137; 1965). Goffman wishes to analyze linguistic behavior as giving individuals *statuses* having certain *rights* and *obligations*. They engage in social routines for various occasions down to the individual *encounter* and its *speech event*. (Goffman 1963).

One of the most extensive projects is Fishman's study of "language dominance" among the Puerto Ricans in Jersey City (Fishman et al., 1968). He concentrated on the question of "who speaks what language to whom and when", to use the title of one of his articles (1965a). In theoretical discussions Fishman faulted both psychologists and linguists – the first for treating bilingualism as a problem in educational achievement, the linguists for treating it as a problem in interference. Fishman found that context is disregarded in both cases and proposed that codes be studied in relation to people's identification with the community and its language-related values. He suggested a form of microanalysis distinguishing appropriate *domains* involving *networks* of communication, with individuals playing various *roles* in each *situation*.

An interesting proposal of a typology for sociolinguistic classification is that of William Stewart (1968). His criteria were *standardization, autonomy, historicity,* and *vitality,* each treated as a binary feature. By combining these he got a classification into *standard* (positive for all four), *classical* (minus vitality), *artificial* (also minus historicity), *vernacular* (minus standardization), *dialect* (minus standardization, autonomy), *creole* (only vitality) and *pidgin* (minus all four). While these features are not always binary, nor are they always independent of one another, the system offers a useful outline.

In all this work there remains some of the conflict between linguists, who prefer to study a few informants intensively, and sociologists, who prefer to take many informants superficially. I have suggested (1972) that sociolinguists should adapt the concepts of *ecology* to these situations. Like animal or human species, the forms of given languages are shaped to the needs of their environment. When a society no longer needs a particular language, it dies and another takes its place. Against this concept one can consider movements for language maintenance and reform as ecological efforts to control the linguistic environment. It is a pleasure to see a German publication entitled *Studies in Language Ecology* (Enninger and Haynes 1984).

(5) Beside the traditional term *bilingualism,* Charles Ferguson has introduced into sociolinguistic discussion the term diglossia, actually an English variant of the French word *diglossie,* a word for bilingualism. (Ferguson 1959) Under this term he pinpointed a particular form of bilingualism found in certain countries. He observed in four widely separated areas the rivalry of two varieties of the same language, one of which he called "high" (H), the other "low" (L). In Arabic countries the H is Classical Arabic, the L the daily spoken tongue in each Arabic country. In Greece the H is the Katharevousa of the Orthodox Church, while the L is the Dimothike of common usage. In Switzerland the H is standard German, used in writing and some official ceremonies, while the L is Swiss German (Schwitzerdütsch) in its various dialects. In Haiti the H is standard French, while L is Haitian Creole, the popular form of French used in that country. The distinction was between a formal, even ritualized language, used for restricted purposes and an informal, everyday language used for everything else.

While one might discuss and quarrel with some of these identifications, especially in the case of Greek, Fishman proceeded to adopt the terminology, while extending its significance. He dropped the linguist's requirement that the two languages be related varieties, concentrating instead on the societal relationship. He instanced the Jewish communities, in which the unrelated Hebrew and Yiddish perform similar sacred/secular functions, a complementarity. One can then describe the situation in Israel as the elimination of Jewish diglossia by extending L-functions to Hebrew.

Neither Ferguson nor Fishman have included in their definition of diglossia the innumerable cleavages within European and other nations between standardized and dialectal varieties. This is actually one of the most widespread forms of bilingualism or bidialectalism. The standards, as we shall see later, are spread by schools, governments, and media, performing all the functions of an H-language. At the same time the population continues in some degree to speak a dialect, universally regarded as an L-language. I have ventured to suggest *schizoglossia,* in analogy with schizophrenia (Haugen 1962), since all of these situations have all the earmarks of diglossia, a clear H/L dichotomy which involves many speakers who vacillate uncertainly between the two.

(6) Language *shifts* may be either dramatic or gradual, often depending on one's point of view. What may appear as a dramatic shift, e.g. of second-generation immigrants in the United States, may actually be a long-time phenomenon for the individual. The results are often seen in the opposed factors of language *spread* and language *death.* A well-known case of spread is that of the Indo-European family from somewhere in eastern Europe (in or near the Caucasus) to much of western Asia and most of Europe, with its colonies overseas. In that same area many languages have suffered death or near-death during the time of spread. We are poorly informed about the earlier phases of such language shifts.

It is therefore apparent that only by studying shifts in the present can we hope to recapture the social mechanisms that underlie them. It is not so much that the languages spread as that changing social circumstances lead the users of the languages to shift orientation. No population shifts its language simultaneously or in all domains and situations. At the very least a language takes a generation to learn and another to forget the old. This will be a period of bilingualism, which functions as a necessary maintenance of social continuity. Yet, as we have shown earlier, each generation moves imperceptibly out of its childhood into an adult usage, a minor shift which may turn into a major shift if it is required to learn a new language.

(7) The study of folk *attitudes* to language may conveniently be called *ethnolinguistics* and must be recognized as at least a factor in language choice and planning. It appears most blatantly in folk etymologies and may in fact be designated as folklore. My own field work has uncovered admiration for

"book language", but did not usually lead to actual imitation of "educated" speech. In Labov's words, "New Yorkers hear themselves not as they actually sound, but rather in accordance with the norms they acknowledge." (Labov 1966: 474)

An interesting series of experiments by Lambert, known as "matched guises", have been used to elicit attitudes. The same speaker holds forth alternately in two languages, and listeners are asked to judge his character etc. in each. Lambert found that in Canada both French and English listeners rated the English voices higher than the French. He also found good correlation between favorable attitudes to the French and success in learning French. (Lambert et al. 1960 etc.)

The success of modern standard languages like French, English, and German as instruments of national policy has led to the common realization that such a language is a necessary instrument of unity. In smaller countries like Iceland the national language is identified with national survival. Nineteenth century Norway and twentieth century Israel are examples of countries struggling to create unity through language. We shall consider these problems in a later chapter.

(8) The *uses* of sociolinguistics offered by Bright (1966) are its value "as a diagnostic index of social structure," "the explanation of historical change," and "the language planner of policy."

Social structure as seen by the sociolinguist is broken up into a complex picture of networks of communication among the holders of certain social positions playing a variety of roles in each domain of social life. An example is the study of pronominal uses in America and Europe by Brown, Gilman, and Ford (1961) and in Russia by Friedrich (1966). I have offered a short survey of Norwegian pronominal usage (see below).

Historical change is ultimately due to the social transmission of language to every new child. The changes in conditions of learning as the child matures will also bring changes in language.

Language planning and its policies are a topic of concern in the analysis of society and its efforts to find a common medium of communication. Problems involving the role of language minorities call for wise planning. American efforts since 1968 to create bilingual programs may be inadequate, but they are still valuable in their attempts to right old wrongs.

Chapter 9

Pluralism: A National Goal?

Language pluralism is not precisely the same as language diversity. The latter is an objective fact of life to be measured by census takers and sociologists (e.g. Lieberson et al. 1974, 1975a,b). It is a fact, for example, that in Nigeria, a former British protectorate, more than two hundred different native languages and dialects are spoken. That is language diversity with a vengeance, and it is hardly a desirable goal for any country that is to have a viable government or a successful school system. When we speak of "pluralism," we imply not a state of affairs, but a goal that may make it possible for diverse language groups to live together. It is a more subjective term, implying a policy of deliberate planning and official action. The very suffix of the word, "-ism," implies that it is a doctrine, a theory, in short a goal that some desire and others deplore. (Berry 1974).

Most people take for granted the language into which they are born, the one spoken in their home and by their playmates. They learn it as a matter of course, and it appears to be of no more consequence to them than the air they breathe. Yet without either one they could not grow up to be human beings. Lack of air would kill their bodies, but lack of language would kill their minds. The language or languages we speak are the result of a long history involving not only ourselves and our ancestors, but our ethnic group and our nation. One part of this history is a set of policies and decisions made far away and long ago without our knowledge and certainly without our consent. Similarly, we who are alive today may by our decisions and our policies be able to influence the lives of those who come after us.

The issue as it is presented to us today is one of centralism and assimilation versus coexistence and pluralism. On every hand the steamroller of uniformation is wiping out ethnic groups and their languages through the spread of national and international languages by radio and TV. But we also see new nations coming into being, struggling to create or preserve their own national languages. They are following the example of the old nations that threw off the yoke of Latin, the world language of western Europe until the sixteenth century (and later).

Today we see within nation after nation a struggle on the part of minorities to assert their linguistic rights: the Catalonians in Spain, the Basques in Spain and France, the Welsh in England, the Lapps (Sami) in Scandinavia, the Chinese in Malaysia, even the Quechua Indians in Paraguay (Rubin 1968).

This struggle between dominated and dominant groups is part of the ecology of language (Haugen 1972). The preservation of language is a part of human ecology.

Although the study of language is the special province of linguists, the ecological struggle involves also a psychological, social, and political problem. Just as we now have a biophysics and a social anthropology, so we have a psycholinguistics and (as we have seen above) a sociolinguistics. There is even a society of "Geolinguistics," the title of a new journal where I found an inspiring article on "linguistic imperialism" by Allen Walker Read (Read 1974).

We shall discuss the problem of how language diversity arose, what policies nations have adopted to meet the problem, and whether a policy of linguistic pluralism can be implemented to solve it.

First the origin of diversity. We must face the fact that most nations have been established by military conquest (or defense) and without regard for the language of their masses. When President Wilson tried after World War I to implement a policy of linguistic self-determination in Europe, it may have been the first time in history that statesmen were called on to pay attention to the wishes of their subjects in such matters. As it turned out, it was largely implemented to break up the Austro-Hungarian empire and to detach the Baltic countries from Russia. But in World War II most of the plan came unstuck. Except for Finland the Baltic countries reverted, and the successor countries to the Austro-Hungarian and Turkish empires, such as Hungary, Romania, Yugoslavia, and Czecho-Slovakia still turned out to be multilingual.

Today it would be hard to name a single European country — except perhaps Iceland — that does not have a minority problem, i.e. a population speaking some language that is more than a dialect of the national tongue. Nations strong enough to extend their power into overseas lands have not hesitated to incorporate populations of different languages and ethnicities. The results are rampant today in the form of internal conflicts at home and colonial collapse abroad. The policy of ethnic incorporation is of course not limited to modern Europe. China, Mongolia, Japan followed it in the Far East, India in South Asia, the Egyptians, the Chaldeans, the Assyrians, anyone you can mention in the Middle and Near East, the Incas and the Aztecs in the Americas, and of course the prehistoric Indo-Europeans. In historical time all major European powers have carried on the Great Tradition of encircling and enslaving racial and lingustic minorities wherever they had the power to do so. Even the small and now pacific Scandinavian nations have a considerable record of linguistic and cultural suppression (on which see below).

Recent years have seen a growing awareness of these problems among social scientists, who previously were either disinterested or hostile. They held minorities to be obstacles to national unity, or in Marxist terms, "a survival of barbarism." In a generally objective study of "ethnic stratification" from 1965, the authors could say that "most Americans who profess humanitarian ideals favor assimilation." (Shibutani and Kwan 1965: 533) They pointed out as an ironic fact that even liberal Americans who condemned "separate but equal" facilities for Blacks and Whites often favored pluralism for European nations. Yet two noted scholars had already published *Beyond the Melting Pot,* in which they had claimed that "the ethnic group in American society" had become "not a survival from the age of mass immigration but a new social form." (Glazer and Moynihan 1963a: 16). The same scholars, in a book entitled *Ethnicity,* maintained that ethnicity is "no mere survival but intimately and organically bound up with major trends of modern societies" (Glazer and Moynihan 1963b: 39; idem, 1975).

Other social theorists have suggested reasons for the survival of minorities in modern societies. Schermerhorn (1964: 238) has suggested the two dimensions of "cultural distinctiveness" and "some form of subjection." This is one way of saying that a minority group need not be a minority: it is really a euphemism for a dominated group. As Blalock (1967: 111) points out, even such a group has its resources of power, if it wishes to achieve certain goals.

One of the resources available either to the elite or the minority is language, both as *symbol* and as *instrument.* One form of social planning is what I have chosen to call *language planning.* There has been an element of that in the Europe of yesterday as in the Africa and Asia of today. We shall look at the theory of language planning in a later chapter. Here we may suggest that it can be either *overt* or *covert, official* or *private.* In reading about the development of English one often gets the impression that like Topsy, it "just grew." But this is an illusion. Guidance may have been covert and private, and still rigidly enforced.

To look at some actual examples, let us begin with Spain, which was not only one of the first great colonizing powers, but also one that had a clear and firm policy about language. The first grammar of a modern language was Nebrija's codification of Castilian, presented to Queen Isabella by her biographer in 1492, the very year in which Columbus discovered America. It was billed as an "instrument of empire," and it established the language of her court as the elite language, at the expense of such other Spanish dialects as those of León and Navarra, as well as the more deviant Galician and Catalonian. Isabella unhesitatingly imposed Castilian on all her subjects, including the Moors. In 1536 Emperor Charles V even ventured to address the Pope in Castilian instead of Latin. The day of Latin was passing and like the Romans the Spaniards were about to make their language the language of their empire (Heath 1972, 1974: 16).

The conquistadores got their instructions in the Laws of Burgos (1512) which required them to train the Indians in the Catholic faith and the Castilian tongue. Eventually this task proved too burdensome for these men of affairs and they turned it over to the friars, with varying effect. But the empires which Spain destroyed, those of the Aztecs in Mexico and the Incas in Peru, had already established and spread their own languages, Nahuatl and Quechua respectively, so the friars often found it simpler to learn these languages and teach Christianity to the natives in their own tongues. By the time of independence in the early nineteenth century, the Latin-American nations had established the supremacy of Spanish without having taught it to all their Indian subjects. Spanish (and in Brazil Portuguese) was the language of the elite, and not until the late 1930's did Mexico begin to institute bilingual education programs as a measure against illiteracy.

The English policy in North America was not basically different from the Spanish, although the attitudes were rather different. In the words of Shirley Brice Heath, "The English viewed language as the mark of an individual's reward of a proper birth or successful educational and social achievements mixed with a careful consciousness about language." (Heath 1974: 9) A little less respectfully: to an Englishman his language was a badge of status. The great turning point for English came with the defeat of the Spanish Armada in 1588, which gave England undisputed mastery of the seas. The language policy was covert and private: language was a personal issue. You were either born to it or you achieved it, and it was not the government's business to prescribe it.

In the eighteenth century distinguished English men of letters, such as Defoe and Swift, urged the foundation of an English academy after the model of the French. The idea was denounced as a tyranny unworthy of Englishmen by none other than Samuel Johnson, who then turned around and made his own dictionary in 1755. This proved to have the same effect as the French Academy, as an enduring force for the uniformity of the language. In the course of the nineteenth century English virtually replaced Gaelic and Erse in Scotland and Ireland and met resistance only in Wales, where language became a non-conformist weapon. Similarly in the United States, revolutionary defiance of English superiority found its advocate in Noah Webster, whose mild reforms were embodied in his dictionary. Private enterprise won the day.

While the English may have lacked a stated language policy, their attitudes were tinged with moral overtones for the elite dialect. "Proper" English is associated with proper morals, "correct" language with correct behavior, and words like "good" and "bad" are equally applicable to a person's language and his moral character. One might not exactly be thrown in jail for either aspect; one could be and often was frozen out of good society, with consequent loss of jobs and restriction of opportunity. Shaw's *Pygmalion* was not just a comedy, but an Irishman's biting satire on the English attitude to language.

In South America the Castilians simply incorporated the well-organized Indians into their own hierarchy, but in North America the largely hunting and gathering Indians were pushed aside and either destroyed or gathered into reservations. There was no government policy to convert the Indians; this was left to missionary organizatons set up by the churches themselves.

The North American Indians proved unwilling to perform hard manual labor for the colonizers, so that when labor was needed, it was obtained either by trading for slaves from Africa or by enticing European immigrants to fill the vast open spaces of the temperate and subarctic zones of the continent. So long as these immigrants did their work, they were left severely alone to speak as they wished. The Blacks were segregated by color, even after the Civil War, and by that time their original languages had practically been lost and English, albeit in more or less creolized form, had become their language.

The white immigrants were admissible to English society in America as soon as they had seen the light and had given up their own tongues. The major instrument in this process was the universal public school, where the much maligned schoolmarm provided models of "correct" speaking. She not only taught a heterogeneous population the three R's, but also served as a cultural and linguistic missionary among the "barbarian" hordes from Germany, Poland, Norway, Italy, or Russia, who became the backbone of the American labor force. (Leibowitz 1974)

It is undeniable that there are great practical advantages in having only one code in governing a country. From this purely practical point of view we might as well have only one language in the whole world, a solution that has had plenty of advocates. To my mind this is a purely bureaucratic solution, worthy of an efficiency expert, but not of a human being. It fails to take into account the fact that in a lifetime most people have no need to communicate with the whole world. Most people live circumscribed, comfortable lives, where the things that matter take place within their homes, among their friends, and at their jobs. The imposition of another language merely for its national or international advantage is disruptive of the life pattern, leaving peple uprooted, lonely, aggressive, and unsocial.

The solution would rather seem to be a thoughtfully and selectively planned bilingualism, which leaves each of us with a native, homely, familiar everyday language in which we can live and love. Then those of us who need it can learn a language of wider communication that will enable us to travel to the ends of the world if occasion arises. (Haugen 1973b). When it is rightly introduced and taught, and is made to seem desirable by the larger society in which we also live, it is not only not harmful, but mind-expanding and infinitely rewarding.

Any problems in bilingual education must not be sought primarily in the schoolroom. We must look back at the ultimate policies, overt or covert, public or private, of the society itself. It is no problem to immerse English-speaking Canadians in French; they will learn English anyhow. But if parents are opposed or if they are indifferent, bilingualism is bound to fail. Among Latin-American and Indian speakers in the United States we may have not an "additive" bilingualism, but a subtractive one.

Switzerland is a country where no one is trying to homogenize the languages of the population. Each canton has its own language, and the country can survive while maintaining three official (and a fourth "national") language, and its German population has its own Swiss German. It is a truly pluralistic country, because each group is left to live its own life.

Perhaps the moral to all this is that real pluralism requires a degree of segregation, of "separate but equal" facilities. But the cement that holds it all together is the body of bilinguals, who can transcend their own group without denying it.

Chapter 10

Language Planning

A good place to begin is Joshua Fishman's survey in his introduction to *Advances in Language Planning* (1974). He holds that the "major dimensions of language planning" are still those that I proposed in my article "Linguistics and Language Planning[n] (1966b) and my book *Language Conflict and Language Planning* (1966a). He is referring to a four-fold model which I first put into matrix form in 1964 (Haugen 1966). The model consists of (1) selection of norm; (2) codification of norm; (3) implementation; and (4) elaboration. Numbers (1) and (3) are the responsibility of society, while (2) and (4) are accomplished by linguists and writers. This produces the following matrix:

	Norm	Function
Society	(1) Selection	(3) Implementation
Language	(2) Codification	(4) Elaboration

Fishman further notes that the model "has been slightly revised and refined" by Neustupný (1970) by the addition of "cultivation" (Fishman 1974a:16). Fishman has provided harmonization of my model with Neustupný's (1974a: 79). I agree that they lend themselves to harmonization, and I welcome the opportunity to provide my own. I believe that the procedures suggested by Neustupný, as well as those of Rubin (1971: "Evaluation") are provided for and to some extent foreseen within my original scheme. Let me explain that the numbering of my four steps does not mean that they are necessarily successive; they may be simultaneous and even cyclical.

(1) *Selection* or choice is called for only when someone has identified what Neustupný has quite rightly called a *language problem*. Most problems can be identified as the presence of conflicting norms, whose relative status needs to be assigned. This can also be called an *allocation of norms*. It can include a decision to replace English with Irish in Eire; or Yiddish with Hebrew in Israel. The selection may be preceded by lengthy wrangling in public or private, and it may be arrived at by some kind of majority decision. But it may also be decreed by an omnipotent ruler, as when Ataturk in 1924 changed Turkish spelling from Arabic to Roman. It may be resisted, as when Hassidic Jews persist in using Yiddish even in Israel.

Over time a selection may be reversed, as English won out over Norman French. The common feature is that it is performed by society, acting through its leaders. It is a form of *policy planning*, which establishes that a given language norm, be it a single item or a whole language, shall enjoy (or lose) a given *status* in a society. While official government agencies are often involved, we must not limit the term "planning" to such action, as I understand a proposal by Jernudd and Das Gupta (1971). Individuals also make their selections, and they may be followed by voluntary groups, whose practice may become normative for a church, a political party, a province, or even a whole country.

(2) *Codification* may be the work of a single person, who more or less informally and knowledgeably decides to give explicit, usually written, form to the norm he has chosen. It need not be his own: many languages have been codified by outsiders, from missionaries to masters. *Graphization* (Ferguson 1968: 29) is often a first step. In areas where the concept of an alphabet, a syllabary, or a system of ideograms exists, a writing tradition can arise simply by the adaptation of a known system to the new language. In the early centuries of our era the Japanese began writing their language with the ideographic *kanji* of Chinese. In the eighteenth century the Faroese writer Svabo wrote his language for the first time, using the Danish form of the Latin alphabet. Even the simplest graphization requires many decisions and should in principle be done by a competent linguist.

Historically, most linguists came in after the fact. To some degree linguistics owes its existence to the practical services linguists could offer as codifiers of language. They learned to extract and formulate the rules of grammar, a process we may call *grammatication*. From Panini to the present grammars have been prescriptive, certainly the ones used in most schools. Whether they are also scientific depends on the skill of the linguist and the philosophy of the times. Beyond grammatication comes *lexication*, the selection of an appropriate lexicon. This may also involve the assignment of styles and spheres of usage for the words of the language. The typical product of codification has been a prescriptive orthography, grammar, and dictionary.

What the French knew as a *grammaire* or *dictionnaire raisonnée* was not an exact description of a real language, but of an ideal language that one was supposed to learn for admission to the world of learning. It could therefore become an instrument of national policy, a language code corresponding to the civil and religious code. Like these it was of course regularly violated, and the degree of punishment depended on the kind of sanctions enforced by society. The grammarian was a lawgiver, and it was natural that his subject should become an important part of the basic education, the *trivium*. It is significant that grammatical deviations are still popularly known by terms of moral opprobrium: they are "bad," "wrong," "incorrect,", "ugly," or "vulgar." Acceptable forms are "good," "right," "correct," "beautiful," or "cultivated." However meaningless such terms may seem to the scientific linguist, he is just as constrained in his usage of the language by the norms implied in these terms as any other user.

Selection and *codification* appear in the same column because they both involve decisions on *form* and are part of what may be called *policy planning*. They correspond closely to the happy distinction introduced by Kloss (1969: 81-83) between *status planning* (which includes selection) and *corpus planning* (which includes codification).

(3) *Implementation* implies the activity of a writer, an institution, or a government in adopting and attempting to spread the language form that has been selected and codified. Dealing, as we are for the most part, with written language, this is done by producing books, pamphlets, newspapers, and textbooks in the language. Those who have authority over schools or over mass media like newspapers, radio, or television introduce it as a medium of instruction and entertainment or at least as a subject to be taught. Laws and regulations are promulgated to encourage (or discourage) its use.

As long as a small, elite group has a monopoly on education, it is relatively simple to implement a given norm. But the spread of schooling to entire populations in modern times has made the implementation of norms a major educational issue. Nation-states are not necessarily created linguistically homogeneous (though attempts in this direction were made at the 1919 Treaty of Versailles and more recently in India). The range of heterogeneity from a simple Iceland to a complex Nigeria is vast and disturbing. Each nation faces problems of its own.

(4) *Elaboration* is in some ways just a continued implementation of a norm to meet the functions of a modern world. The major languages of Europe have set the standard here by their amazing inventiveness since the time of the Renaissance, when they undertook to replace the functions of Latin. Elaboration is a useful English equivalent of Kloss's German term *Ausbau* (1969); it has been used for a somewhat similar concept by Bernstein (e.g. 1971). A modern language of high culture needs a terminology for all the intellectual and humanistic disciplines, including the sciences, and not to forget the cultural underworld that runs from low to popular.

As far as I can see, the term fully includes whatever is meant by Neustupný's *cultivation approach* (1970: 39; in revised form 1978: 258-268). He suggests that it is either opposed to or added to "language planning" and quite rightly indicates that it is more characteristic of developed than of developing nations. He points out that terms for *cultivation* are a normal part of the terminology in this field in many European nations where it is desired to describe what academies and other guardians of the language claim to be doing.

In creating my model I was of course not unaware of this terminology, which is also well established in the Scandinavian languages: in Swedish (*språk*)*vård*, in Norwegian (*mål*)*rφkt*, Danish (*sprog*)*rφgt*, meaning "care, cultivation", metaphorically drawn from the care of animals and plants, and corresponding to the German (*Sprach*)*pflege*. I included this idea in my term *elaboration*, rejecting *cultivation* as a somewhat elitist view of "culture" and "cultivation". Also, it was not an established or neutral term in English in reference to language. I wished to have a wider term like *language planning* to cover the whole area of language treatment, both for the developing and the developed nations.

Here it may be illuminating to ask what the Swedish Language Committee (*Svenska språknämnden*) actually does in its quarterly publication *Språkvård* (Language Cultivation). It has published a special series of brochures on spelling rules, pronunciation, place names, "right and wrong in language," a guide to the dictionary of the Swedish Academy, word formation, inter-Scandinavian problems, transliterating Russian, the language of the mass media, bureaucratic gobbledygook, technical language, family names, medical terms, and descriptions of several urban idalects. In the periodical there are special articles on these and similar topics, as well as question-and-answer columns on problems of correctness or language history. In short, Swedish as a well-established standard language has a continuing problem of implementation (informing the public) and elaboration (making decisions on novel problem, e.g. what should "plastics" be called?) I suggest that their *cultivation* is that process of continued planning, here summed up as *implementation* and *elaboration*, that goes on in every language once the basic form has been established.

Neustupný has proposed *language treatment* as an overall name for the process. This metaphor to me smacks of the sickroom, a metaphor that is in itself too vague. Once we begin with the identification of a language problem, the natural solution is to make plans. Hence I continue to prefer *language planning*. The term is well established: we have a *Language Planning Newsletter*, a periodical entitled *Language Problems and Language Planning*, and a hefty volume entitled *Advances in Language Planning* (Fishman 1974a), as well as a volume of *References for Students of Language Planning* (Rubin and Jernudd, 1977).

Two other suggested terms may be regarded as valuable supplements to the model and can easily find their places within it. Neustupný's remarks on the need for *correction procedures* are well taken. Some of them are part of the function of parents and agemates in the acquisition of language by the child. They are more consciously applied in school by teachers and through textbooks; eventually they may become self-administered through reading and general social acculturation. The need for *evaluation procedures* (Rubin 1971) is also clear. If we set out to reintroduce Gaelic in Eire, one would hope that we should not forget to provide some way of evaluating the success of our program. All of this is part of any good program of *implementation*, leading to successful listening and reading, or better still, speaking and writing.

For further detail in the discussion of theory I refer to Karam (1974) and the above-mentioned bibliography. The time has come to present a revised model for language planning. In the revision shown below I have incorporated the most important insights of my colleagues without altering the basic outline of my original plan.

Even with this revision I cannot claim that it is a complete theory of language planning (LP). It provides a description of what language planners have done, without identifying precisely why they have done it, nor what goals they have hoped to attain. For some discussion I refer to my 1966 article (Haugen 1966a: 60-64). Prague School theorists (as Garvin has repeatedly told us, cf. Garvin 1973) once proposed as criteria of a standard language that it should be "stable" but also "flexible." This was done in opposition to rhetoricians who saw the ideal as just stable. As he has granted, these properties are really a description of all living languages (Fishman 1974a: 73 note).

The problem is how to build these qualities into a formal standard language. It is like asking a disciplinarian to be both firm and gentle, or telling a mother to spank her children lovingly! How stable and how flexible? Other writers have set up certain ideals for language, e.g. Ray (1963) with his "economy," "rationality," and "commonalty," or Tauli (1968, 1977) who emphasizes "instrumental efficiency." These do not seem to have played much role in the creation of standard languages, though they are fine ideals for language planners to keep in mind (Haugen 1971). The problem is how to apply or define them in such a way that they will convince language planners. Or why do we "practical" Americans use four syllables to say *elevator*, while the "impractical" English do it in one with *lift*?

For the moment our discipline remains largely descriptive and hypothetical, not having reached a stage of "explanatory adequacy." Perhaps it is bound to remain so until we know more about the reasons for *unplanned* change in language. Fishman has called for a theory of language planning, without clarifying just how he thinks such a theory should look. It would surely have to be one that takes a stand on difficult value judgments. We are aware of various ways of writing a language; but it may be difficult to say that one way is better than another. Could we even reach agreement on whether it is better to write alphabetically, syllabically, or ideographically? If alphabetically, should we write phonetically, phonemically, or morphophonemically, and how much weight should we give to tradition and etymology? Where norms conflict, shall we plan for unity or for diversity, for shift or maintenance? Do we like "little" languages, used by small groups, and if so, what are we doing to save them? If we are in favor of "great" languages, which one shall we promote? Or shall we choose one of the several hundred Esperanto-type artificial languages? If ours is a species of cultivation, what species shall we cultivate? If we would cure linguistic ills, what are our remedies?

Table 1. A Revised Model of Language Planning

	Form (policy planning)	Function (cultivation)

Society (Status planning)	1) Selection (decision procedures)
	  a) Identification of problem
	  b) Allocation of norms
		3) Implementation (educational spread)
		  a) Correction procedures
		  b) Evaluation

Language (Corpus planning)	2) Codification (standardization procedures)
	  a) Graphization
	  b) Grammatication
	  c) Lexication
		4) Elaboration (functional development)
		  a) Terminological modernization
		  b) Stylistic development

Chapter 11

Implementation

Language planning has many pitfalls, and one of the most menacing is the difficulty of actually implementing even the most desirable changes, especially in a modern society. In this chapter we shall take up two cases of interest to me and see how they have worked out.

Case 1. *Metrication*. This relates to the trivial but irritating differences between British and American spelling, mostly established by Noah Webster in a burst of nationalistic separation and rationalistic reform. The problem has surfaced in connection with the proposed introduction into the United States of the metric system. The discussion reported below relates to the spelling of the central word: American *meter* or British *metre?*

Most Americans have probably met with the metric system for the first time in a science class. Devised at the time of the French Revolution, it has by this time won acceptance throughout the world, except in the English-speaking countries. Until recently these clung to their feet and inches, quarts and gallons, pounds and miles. It took a world war and its aftermath to lead Britain down the metric path. In 1968 the Congress authorized a survey to study its effects. Three years later an official committee recommended "that the United States change to the International Metric System through a coordinated national program over a period of ten years . . ." (De Simone 1971: 85). The report was appropriately subtitled: "A Decision Whose Time has Come."

In 1975 the Congress adopted a Metric Conversion Act calling for voluntary conversion to the metric system (Public Law 94-168). Some effects began appearing in the form of occasional metric signs on our roads, designations on our products, and temperatures in our weather programs. Just how or when the conversion will actually take place is unclear. Not surprisingly, it is slow: I note that in France it took 45 years (1795-1840) before it was fully accepted. Against a background of our need to buy and sell abroad it seems inevitable.

In 1971 the National Bureau of Standards in Washington issued an official translation of a French document on the international units of the system (NBS Special Publication 330). This document presents the units adopted at a conference in Paris in 1960. The English translation came in separate versions for Britain and the United States, the latter being edited by Chester H. Page of the NBS. It showed the basic unit as *metre* (and presumably *litre*); it was understood that a "gentleman's agreement" had been made whereby the U.S. would accept *-re* in *metre* as a quid pro quo for Britain's giving up the *-me* on *kilogramme.*

I do not know whether Dr. Page was aware of the hornet's nest he would stir up, but several American scientists at once spotted the deviation from the traditional American spelling. Here was indeed a "conflict of norms" that called for "corpus planning": a novel codification had been selected. At least two of the English spellings that Webster rejected have crept into limited American usage: *theatre* and *glamour* (for *glamor*). The former is used in many theaters, the latter in perfume ads. The snob appeal of these spellings consists in equal parts of anglo- and francophile sentiment. But in the case of *metre* and *litre* we are dealing with an area of hard-headed, scientific practice, as well as one that will affect the daily lives of every American who buys a liter of milk or a meter of cloth. All available American dictionaries designate the spellings with *-re* as "chiefly British."

One scientist who leaped into action was Dr. John Howard, editor of *Applied Optics,* journal of the Optical Society of America. In an editorial in his issue for August 1971 he reported that at a meeting of the Publication Board of the American Institute for Physics "the editors of all the physics journals vote overwhelmingly not to yield the phonetic spelling of meter, liter, diopter in any such compromise with evil." He was frank to say that the British spellings "rankled" and caused hackles to rise. "Our gram, meter, and ton are all more phonetic and logical than gramme, metre, and tonne, and we should not retreat from any phonetic spellings just because the British have multiple errors." Dr. Howard continued to beat the drum in his editorials for at least four years — I have ten of them down to 1975, but there may be more.

I should add that Dr. Howard, although an optical engineer, admits to having taken college courses in the older Germanic languages, including Old and Middle English and Old High German (personal communication, June 20, 1974). Another active opponent of the British spellings came from Canada, rather surprisingly in view of Canada's having adopted *-re.* Albert Mettler, secretary of the Canadian Metric Association, put up a strong argument for *-er* in a *Metric Fact Sheet* of 1974.

My connection with the problem came through a former student of mine, Susan P. Bryant, who worked for Dr. Bruce Barrow, then of Waltham, Massachusetts. He was a member of the Standards Committee of the Institute of Electrical and Electronics Engineers, which had set up an American National Metric Council with offices in Washington, which in turn had a Metric Practice Committee. In the fall of 1973 Dr. Barrow was made chairman of a Task Force on Spelling and Pronunciation which brought in a preliminary draft presenting arguments on both sides of the spelling controversy. In a poll of American scientists the vote was three to one in favor of the American spellings.

Dr. Barrow decided to consult professional linguists and Ms. Bryant suggested that he turn to me. I first heard of it in a letter of January 21, 1974, to which I replied, supporting his view in favor of the American spellings. I argued on the grounds of (1) usage (*-re* would confuse learners and bring resistance to metrication); (2) national unity (we might risk a splitting whereby the scientific community would write *-re* and the average layman *-er*); (3) phonology (syllabic *r* is spelled *er* in both British and American usage in the overwhelming majority of words); (4) morphology (derivatives in a consonant followed by *-r-* usually have bases in *-er*, e.g. *fibrous* from *fiber*, *diametrical* from *diameter*, *disastrous* from *disaster*, *hungry* from *hunger* etc. For the attainment of a unified spelling in English, it would make better sense for the less numerous community (Great Britain) to adopt the more rational spelling than for the more numerous one to adopt a less rational spelling.

Rather than depend on my (possibly biased) views alone, however, I recommended consultation with leading authorities on American English, specifically Frederic Cassidy of the University of Wisconsin, Albert Marckwardt of the University of Michigan, and Rudolph Troike of the Center for Applied Linguistics. Troike brought in other linguists, including Professor Randolph Quirk from England. The opinion was absolutely unanimous in favor of *-er*. We learned that in 1926 the old guardian of the Queen's English, H. W. Fowler, had admitted that "the American usage is . . . more consistent . . . But we prefer in England to break with our illogicalities slowly" (Fowler 1926). In Sir Ernest Gower's revision of Fowler (1965) it is admitted that words like *hexameter, diameter,* and *perimeter* are regularly written *-er* and that *kilometer* is so written more often than not.

A revised draft (dated September 5, 1974) was written, incorporating the opinions of the linguists and the poll of the scientists. This led the Board of Directors of the Metric Council to change its policy (March 20, 1975). Shortly after this the Department of Commerce issued notices advising all government agencies to write *-er*. In 1977 a new version of NBS Special Paper 330 was issued, changing *-re* to *-er*.

This is not quite the end of the story. The editor of the *Newsletter* of the United States Metric Association, one Louis Sokol of Boulder, Colorado, issued a spirited attack on the advocates of *-er* in 1975. He followed it up with a brochure entitled *Statement on the Spelling of Metre* (1978).

Mr. Sokol accused the advocates of *-er* as taking "a chauvistinic attitude" and trying to "impose their will on the English-speaking world" after the fashion of the "ugly American" (1978: 6-8). He was liberal in his use of pejorative adjectives, describing his opponents as "vociferous" and "retrogressive." The linguists are said to have violated "one of the principal ethics of a linguist" which is "a linguist does not prescribe a language, he describes it" (1978: 7). Nevertheless, he brings in his own linguists, Allan R. Taylor of the University of Colorado, a specialist on American Indian languages, and Morris Halle of M.I.T. The former declared that the problem is trivial, that both spellings are phonetically adequate, that any literate person will recognize both, and that the question is purely political and sociological, hence pragmatic and nonlinguistic. Neither linguist has ever shown any interest in language planning, but of course there is merit in their argument.

We will not pursue the problem further. As language planners we may well be perplexed: shall our *selection* be national or international? Shall English *codification* follow the Germanic principle of writing *-er* (which in this case is also Latin and Greek) or shall it preserve a French spelling for historical and sentimental reasons? Shall the *implementation* be imposed by a private scientific organization or by a department of the United States government? Is all this purely political, as Taylor claims, or do linguists have a contribution to make?

Case 2. *Editing Out Sexism.* A body of functionaries who exert an enormous and probably growing influence on the shape of American expository prose is the editorial staffs employed by American publishers. Most of them are women, well trained in the arts of rhetoric, and personally delightful. However painless they try to make the process, having one's manuscript edited by one of them is like nothing so much as going to the dentist.

For English language planning it would be a most interesting and significant research project to study just exactly what they do in implementing what they understand to be the codification of standard English. It must of course be realized that they are slaves to whatever style manual is adopted by their organization, whether it be the University of Chicago Style Manual or that of the Modern Language Association, which I understand has grown from a slim pamphlet to a big book. We are happy as long as they limit themselves to appropriate punctuation, to catching slips in spelling and grammatical coherence, and to eliminating anacolutha. Having been an English major myself and having some experience in writing, I dream of some day writing a book in which the editors will find no elementary errors to correct. But when I write "epochmaking" in one word, I get it back hyphenated; if I hyphenate "step-sister," it comes back solid. Numbers below hundred must be written out, but this does not apply to percentages. If I write "that" as a relative pronoun, it gets changed to "which" and vice versa. While my pronouns seem crystal clear to me, they are often replaced by nauseatingly repetitive nouns. Editors replace my conjunction "while" with "though" because there is a rule that "while" should be temporal (although the dictionary records both). My sentence adverbs are forever being shifted around, especially "only" and "here."

But their special *bête noir* is my attempt to keep my style colloquial. If I write that someone "decides to stick it out" or that two writers "were running neck and neck," these phrases are slashed or questioned.

My latest experience in the field brought me up short before a solid wall of feminism. I was of course aware of the flurries over "chairperson" and the sexist gender system of Indo-European, but I had not realized that there is already a set of guidelines adopted as a policy by some of our presses. Maija Blaubergs of the University of Georgia, an educational psychologist, has kindly enlightened me and furnished me with two of her papers (1978a, 1978b).

I have been struck by the interest of this movement for students of language planning. In her earlier article she lists some of the recommended devices for avoiding sexist terms: circumlocutions, indefinite and plural pronouns, sex-neutral nouns and affixes, creating new terms, and avoiding such common idioms as "man overboard," "good will to men," and "man's best friend." In her later article she reports on some "misconstructions" placed on sex-neutral language planning, including cases of ridiculous over-extension. I think my favorites of this type are the replacements of "hysterectomy" by "herterectomy" and of "hernia" with "hisnia."

To return to my own experience: I had thought of myself as quite un-chauvinistic and had provided liberally for "his and her" in my text. But to my shame I had written of "a poet who tries to reach his audience"; the "his" had to go for "an" audience. I had said that he wrote "for all mankind"; but when this was systematically changed to "humankind," I boggled and adopted "humanity" instead. Without intending to write a religious tract, I had said that "Jesus proclaimed that all men were sinful." Even sin we men cannot have to ourselves: I had to make it sex-neutral, I suppose "people" or "persons."

My embarrassment was the greater since the book dealt with the dramatist who wrote the drama of women's liberation a century ago, Ibsen's *A Doll's House* (Haugen 1979). As will appear in a later chapter, I had recently publish-ed a squib on "sexism" in the Norwegian language (Haugen 1977), reporting on the fact that even so, Norwegian women are (like American women) rebelling against the built-in chauvinisms of their language. My view there was that social discrimination may be reflected in language, but is neither caused by it nor seriously influenced by changes in it. Norwegian nurses have adopted the masculine form of their professional title (*sykepleier*, rejecting the traditional *sykepleierske*). But Swedish nurses have gone the opposite way, retaining the feminine (*sjuksköterska*), apparently because the masculine (*sjukskötare*) would lower their status to that of an attendant in a mental institution (Andersson 1976). A news dispatch reported that the Wives Coalition of the Pacific Coast Fishermen vigorously protested the U.S. Commerce Department's change of their husbands from "fisherman" to "fisher." (Fleming 1979)

No one can doubt that a social and generational change is taking place here and in other Western countries in the position of women. The important thing is to eliminate all forms of negative discrimination against women. I am in favor of discrimination so long as it is positive. In any case we are clearly in the midst of a process of language planning. Women have identified a language problem, namely that traditional language conflicts with their desired role in society. So they wish to make a new selection and codification, and some of them are actually implementing and elaborating it. As with all innovations, many of the proposals will disappear as fashions change. Hopefully only the best will remain.

Chapter 12

Semicommunication

The fragmentation of Scandinavia is a reflection of its political history. One is tempted to say that Scandinavia is more balkanized than the Balkans. It is a miniature Europe, with all the minority problems that beset other parts of the world. The problems as well as the solutions may be more transparent in a smaller sample.

An American headline recently described Scandinavia as "five nations in search of a mother tongue." Except for the fact that they are not really in search of it, this is an apt observation. The fragmentation exists within an overall cultural unity in which language plays a major role. What Scandinavians call *Norden* — the North — consists of five sovereign nations, three central (Denmark, Norway, Sweden), two marginal (Iceland, Finland). Between them they have six official standard languages of Germanic origin (from west to east: Icelandic, Faroese, Nynorsk-Norwegian, Bokmål-Norwegian, Danish, Swedish) and one of Finno-Ugric origin (Finnish).

The four central languages are mutually intelligible (with a little good will) and in practice they function as dialects of a common Scandinavian "language" (Braunmüller 1979). They are *Ausbau* languages in Kloss's terminology (1978), i.e. languages by virtue of separate standardizations. Finnish is clearly an *Abstand* language, while Faroese and Icelandic are somewhere between, being akin to the others, but in general unintelligible. Within the central area there are also mutually unintelligible dialects, which may even share features with other languages than their own. The national borders are determined by past historical conflicts, in which military power was more significant than linguistic self-determination. (For surveys see Haugen 1976a, Sigurd ed. 1977, Bandle 1979).

Scandinavians are no doubt more aware than the citizens of larger countries of their vulnerable position. The well-known linguist Hans Vogt, addressing a congress of linguists in Reykjavik, reminded them that the Nordic countries are "small language societies which, in a world that is constantly being more and more internationalized and standardized, are exposed to increasing pressure from the outside world, from the great languages of culture" (Vogt 1970).

We shall consider the influence of English in a later chapter; it is a matter of deep concern to many (Sutton 1979). The first foreign language introduced was Latin. Christian missionaries of the tenth and eleventh centuries accomplished what Roman legions had failed to do. The first schools were Latin schools, in which clerics not only trained new clerics, but also budding bureaucrats for the royal chanceries. In so doing, they brought Scandinavia within the orbit of European culture, at the same time depriving the vernaculars of part of their natural domain. They set up a functional diglossia, with Latin as the "high" (H) language and the vernaculars as the "low" (L) languages. (Ferguson 1959)

Even so, the Scandinavian languages were written in Roman letters on parchment by these same missionaries and clerics, less so in the East than in the West, where Christianity was introduced from the British Isles. It is characteristic that the Danish Saxo Grammaticus (fl. c. 1200) wrote his history of Denmark in Latin, while his Icelandic contemporary, Snorri Sturluson (1178-1241) wrote his history of Norway in the vernacular. Latin was more than a link with Europe. In the words of Sigmund Skard: "In certain areas of life the use of Latin soon became a matter of course" (Skard 1980: 29)

The Reformation may be regarded as the first minority revolt against the dominance of Latin. By rejecting the authority of the Roman Church and introducing the vernacular into the service, the Germanic nations at one blow eliminated one of the major domains of Latin. In the sixteenth century, after the model of Luther, the Nordic nations not only established national churches, but also translated the Bible into the vernaculars: primarily Swedish (1541) and Danish (1550), secondarily Icelandic (1584) and Finnish (New Testament 1548).

Even after the Reformation Latin remained a window to the world. Humanism established Latin as the language of learning. As Skard once more puts it: "Latin became a mark of social standing, the insurmountable barrier between the cultured and others." (Skard 1980: 57) The gradual restriction of Latin began in the Middle Ages: Queen Margaret of Denmark issued her first law in Danish in 1396. (Tengström 1973; Wennås (1966).

By this time another language was threatening Scandinavian autonomy, the Low German of northern Germany. This language was spread by the powerful Hanseatic League, by the involvement of the Danish and Swedish courts with German rulers and noblemen, and by the influx of thousands of German craftsmen and merchants to the cities of the North. According to Skautrup, historian of Danish, between 1325 and 1425 Denmark was well on its way to becoming bilingual in German and Danish (Skautrup 2.31). At one time the kingdom of Denmark embraced so many speakers of German that they constituted one third of its entire population (Brems 1979: 428). In 1864 Germany retrieved most of the German population as well as some Danes, who were returned to Denmark after World War I (1920). The border is ragged and there are still small minorities on both sides of it (Søndergård 1978, 1980).

Around 1700 the linguistic situation was such that a later Danish writer, Wilster, could describe it as follows:
Each man who went deep into learning
On paper wrote nothing but Latin,
Spoke French to his ladies, German to dogs,
And Danish only to servants.
By 1700 the new standards for Danish and Swedish had been firmly established, i.e. codified and implemented. Their complete victory with full elaboration would not come until the nineteenth century, when universal school systems were established for the teaching of the native languages. These norms were strikingly different from the written norms of the Middle Ages. At that time Scandinavia was briefly united under Danish hegemony and Danish had a fleeting chance to become the standard language of all Scandinavia (as it did in fact in Norway). But the Swedish secession of 1523 under king Gustavus Vasa meant that Danish supremacy found a formidable rival. As late as 1506 prominent Swedes could humbly acknowledge that they and the Danes were "all of one language," but by 1554 they had discovered that the Danes "do not trouble to speak like other people, but force their words out as if they wish to cough." (Haugen 1976a: 326).

When the Swedes in the sixteenth century established their official norm, they made it as different as possible from Danish. After 1658 they instituted a policy euphemistically known as *uniformiteten* (the uniformity) in the formerly Danish and Norwegian provinces of western and southern Sweden. In one generation they turned the written language of these provinces from Danish to Swedish, without much effect on the local speech (Ingers 1974, Ohlsson 1978-9).

The most striking feature of the new Danish and Swedish norms alike (and of Norwegian dialects) was their formal departure from the norms of the old languages. Having ridden out the threat of Latin and Low German, they ended by absorbing many of their features. They were flooded by thousands of Low German and Latin loanwords. The old synthetic grammatical structure with many suffixes and relatively free word order had changed into an analytical morphology with few suffixes and relatively rigid word order. The leap was similar to that from Old to New English, and it is not fanciful to attribute the change in part to foreign influence: in Scandinavia Low German, in England French. What the Norman Conquest did for English, the Hanseatic dominance did for Scandinavian. Only in Iceland has the old structure and much of the old lexicon survived; it is as if an Anglo-Saxon-speaking community had survived in England.

Once these new norms had been established by the combined forces of government and church, with the schools and the printing press as new and powerful instruments, it was only a matter of time until they had become the chief means of unification within their respective realms. The process was completed in the nineteenth century, when the entire population was gradually mobilized into more or less active participation in the lives of the nations.

The French Revolution and the Napoleonic wars created new political alignments that shook the established positions of Danish and Swedish. In 1809 Finland was lost to Sweden; in 1814 Norway was lost to Denmark. Movements for linguistic autonomy arose in Finland and Norway, partly influenced by the ideology of the Romantic Movement. By the middle of the century similar movements gathered force in Iceland and the Faroes, eventually bringing independence for Iceland (1918, 1944) and home rule for the Faroes (1948). In the modern period we also observe the establishment of active organs for language cultivation, the best known being the Swedish Academy of 1786. Its purpose was declared to be to work for "the purity, strength, and sublimity" of Swedish, but it is not clear just how much it actually contributed to these laudable goals. By the end of the nineteenth century, at least, the maintenance and cultivation of the norms were actually in the hands of the ministries of education of the respective nations, under advice from *ad hoc* committees of linguistic and pedagogical specialists.

(a) Finland: In the Swedish kingdom Finnish was a minority language, demographically and functionally. The tables were turned in 1809 when Finland became a Grand Duchy under Russia, with considerable autonomy. The national epic, the *Kalevala,* pieced together by Elias Lönnrot (1835), became a symbol of nationality. Elaboration followed as Finnish was encouraged to take over new functions. Although Swedish Finns continued to exist and were the old elite, their proportions and their influence diminished. The administration became bilingual, but by 1980 the core population of Swedish speakers was no more than 6.4 per cent of the total population. Across the border in northern Sweden, in the valley of Tornedalen, a population of Finns found themselves on the wrong side of the border. Until recently the Swedish government either ignored them or tried to assimilate them. After more than a century of melting-pot treatment, the people of Tornedalen are enjoying a belated taste of schooling in the language many of them still use in daily life. (Hansegård 1968; Wande 1977).

(b) Iceland: In the late eighteenth and early nineteenth centuries Icelandic was recodified from the half-Danicised language of the 1584 Bible by reference to the classic models from Old Icelandic. It was the good fortune of the Icelanders to have maintained a strong literary tradition, and to live remote from the mainland, and to lack urban centers of linguistic influence. The enthusiasm of Nordic and German scholars stimulated the Icelanders to undertake a program of corpus planning that would save them from the leveling out of the mainland languages. Icelandic became a model and an inspiration for others, especially in the Faroes and in Norway.

(c) The Faroes: While Icelandic only needed to be rediscovered, Faroese had to be created out of the spoken dialects of the islands. The first language planner was the fabulous but neglected J.C. Svabo, who used a Danish-based orthography to transcribe its vast treasure of dance ballads (1773 ff.). But it acquired a truly national orthography from V. U. Hammershaimb (1846), who codified the language to make it resemble Icelandic as much as possible. The result has been an enduring but phonetically frustrating norm. It can be said that it is no one's speech, but everyone's language. We shall return to Faroese below.

(d) Norway: No new Norwegian standard was created while Norway was united with Denmark; the post-Reformation writers learned to write an acceptable Danish. In the course of time a new Norwegian speech norm arose, in part dependent on written Danish. Its existence as "cultivated daily speech" in the urban and bureaucratic classes was not recognized until the 1840's, when it was identified and advocated as the basis of a reformed orthography by Knud Knudsen.

Also in the 1840's an alternative norm was proposed by Ivar Aasen, more along the lines of Hammershaimb's Faroese. As Norway's first dialectologist, he collected information from field work throughout the country. On the basis of his findings he compiled a grammar and a dictionary of a language he envisaged as the future Norwegian. It was a masterpiece of language planning, establishing a norm that was recognizable as genuinely Norwegian, yet not a return to Old Norwegian.

Aasen's language came to be known as *Landsmaal* ("Countrywide Language") and is now called *Nynorsk* ("New Norwegian"). Knudsen's language came to be known as *Riksmaal* ("State Language") and is now called *Bokmål* ("Book Language") or by some *Riksmål*. Under nationalistic influence inspired by opposition to the Swedish union, both Norwegian languages were recognized in 1885 and left to fight it out. Today they have grown closer together, but the Dano-Norwegian (*Bokmål*) is still dominant over the New Norwegian, which has only about 16 per cent of the school districts. It is even questionable whether they should now be recognized as distinct languages; they function more as dialects.

(e) Marginal Minorities. In their zeal to establish norms, the Scandinavians of the nineteenth century showed little concern for the marginal or semi-colonial speech groups. Greenland housed an Eskimo population which became a part of the Danish kingdom. Hans Egede became a missionary for their conversion; his son Paul wrote the first grammar in 1760 and translated the New Testament in 1766. The modern orthography is the work of a German, Samuel Kleinschmidt (1814-1886). Only recently, with the home rule act of 1979, have the Greenlanders begun to develop a fully functional language.

The Lapps, or Sami, as they now wish to be known, occupy the northern provinces of Norway, Sweden, Finland, and Soviet Russia. They have been treated as children of nature, much like our Indians, picturesque but primitive. The language problem is exacerbated by the splitting among nations and by its own dialectization. Since 1956 there has been a Nordic Sami Council, active in creating textbooks and other tools for the preservation of the language.

The Romany or Gypsy population tends to be peripatetic, and for the most part they ask only to be left alone. The old Indic tribe, which has been in Scandinavia at least since 1500, still speak Romany, but often in a debased form as a secret vocabulary within the framework of the local idiom.

(f) Immigrants. The most recent and probably the most acute minority problem is the one created here as elsewhere by the immigration of exiles and laborers. Children with home languages from Italy and Spain to Turkey and Pakistan are faced with school systems that are geared to teach only Scandinavian. Special research projects have been set up to study the problem, and books as well as periodicals have appeared to resolve them.

(g) Dialects. In later years there have been rumblings of discontent over the enforcement of national standards in school to the detriment of local dialects. As long ago as 1961 Tore Österberg, a teacher in northern Sweden, wrote a dissertation on the problems faced by his pupils. He advocated that they be given materials to read composed in their own dialect. A movement in this direction has been strongest in Norway, where the New Norwegian movement has especially encouraged it.

So far I have deliberately stressed the centrifugal trends: one minority after another is knocking on the doors of the language. But there are also movements in favor of Nordic unity. In 1978 a Nordic Language Board was established, including even Greenlandic and Sami representatives, as well as all the standards so far discussed. Special efforts of teaching and publication are being encouraged to prevent the central languages from drifting apart and to keep the marginal languages alive.

Chapter 13
Interlanguage

The problem of Scandinavian intercommunication is of interest since it is typical of a number of similar situations in various parts of the world. My own concern with it arose from personal experience since boyhood with meeting occasional Danes and Swedes among the friends of my Norwegian family. Visits to Scandinavia in my adult years as professor of Scandinavian whetted my interest. In Copenhagen I once sought out Professor Sven Clausen, not a linguist but a professor of jurisprudence, because of his interesting campaign on behalf of greater understanding among Scandinavians. From 1937 to 1948 he agitated on behalf of changes in Danish that might keep the language in closer touch with Swedish and Norwegian. He was serious in his intentions, but could be quite amusing in his methods, being also a successful playwright. The scenario he developed for "cleansing" Danish was a regular program of language planning. On the occasion of my visit he had concluded his campaign and generously gave me whatever I wanted of his literature on the subject. (Clausen 1938ff.)

One result was that I undertook what turned out to be a pioneer investigation of Scandinavian opinion on the topic by means of written questionnaires. With the assistance of the society Norden I mailed out 300 questionnaires to addressees in each of the three central Scandinavian countries, randomly chosen from the national telephone catalogs.

The questions to which I sought answers were of the following types: How great is the actual contact between the Nordic peoples? Which social classes are especially interested in Nordic cooperation? What are the most common misunderstandings and difficulties arising between Scandinavians? How great is the interest in these problems in each country? What is being done to overcome the obstacles that exist and how effective are these efforts? What more can be done that is not being done today?

The results from the 28 per cent of replies actually received were interesting and significant. One can read my conclusions in various published articles (Haugen 1953b, 1966c). Briefly stated, they were that Nordic cooperation was largely of interest to the academic and upper middle class; that Danes show the greatest interest and Swedes the least; that conscious efforts to modify the languages have been largely unsuccessful; that individuals are torn between loyalty to their particular language and a desire to encourage inter-Scandinavian cooperation; that further research is imperative.

It should not be overlooked that in response to Clausen's agitation the Danish government did adopt some minor changes in Danish spelling. These immediately made the language more easily accessible, at least for Norwegian readers. The originally German practice of capitalizing nouns was abandoned and the writing of å for aa was adopted. On the other hand, the public use of slang has tended to obscure understanding.

It took a new generation of Scandinavian linguists to pick up my challenge and add new materials to the study of inter-Nordic relations. In the meanwhile each country had created its own language commission, with Nordic cooperation as one of its declared goals. For an account of their early history see the Swedish commission's ten-year jubilee issue, *Språkvård* (1954).

In 1976 Øivind Maurud published a study of mutual intelligibility among the Nordic languages, followed by an essay by Stig Örjan Ohlsson (1979). Both were published under the auspices of the Nordic Council, an inter-Scandinavian parliamentary organization. Maurud calls my investigation "a praiseworthy effort" and regrets that it was not followed up. Ohlson calls it "a pioneering work," though methodologically inadequate.

Maurud's study improves greatly on my statistics. He bases his work on tests given to an equal number of recruits in each of the three countries (84). As a well-trained educational psychologist he operates with indices of reliability and validity. He also distinguished sharply between oral and written competence (in understanding). He found that Norwegians understood Danish and Swedish better than Danes and Swedes understood each other or Norwegian. Also that written text was better understood than spoken. Finally that Norwegians understood Swedish better than Danish. There are various weaknesses in his test, e.g. that most of the recruits proved to be from areas around the national capitals, so that for example more Norwegians could hear Swedish TV than vice versa.

While Maurud is a Norwegian, Ohlsson is a Swede. He gave a historical survey, including a discussion of the role of the media, such as a proposed transmission of programs by satellite. In 1977 the Nordic Council was moved to take a further step:it proposed the creation of a Nordic Language Secretariat. Its function would be to coordinate all the Scandinavian language commissions and work to protect and strengthen Nordic solidarity and promote Nordic intelligibility. (Nordiskt språksekretariat 1977). The secretariat was established in 1978 in Oslo, with Ståle Løland, a Norwegian, as its secretary and Bertil Molde of Sweden as its president. Under its auspices a conference on Internordic Intelligibility (*språkforståelse*) was held in Umeå, Sweden, in 1981 (Elert 1981). The first publication of the Secretariat was a book surveying the languages of Scandinavia, which now had risen to eight – the Indo-European Danish, Faroese, Icelandic, Norwegian, and Swedish; the Eskimo Greenlandic; and the Finno-Ugric Finnish and Samish. (Molde and

Karker 1983). The Secretariat also took over the publication of *Språk/ Sprog i Norden* 1983, which had been appearing in one form or another since WW II. New prospects of Nordic cooperation were being opened up at the highest level.

While Scandinavians like to think of their situation, which I have called "semicommunication", as quite unique, it is not difficult to find parallels elsewhere. The relation between Czech and Slovak in Czecho-Slovakia, between Serbian and Croatian in Yugoslavia, or Macedonian and Bulgarian can be instanced. In the Arab world there are parallels, and of course in India between Hindi and Urdu.

Such problems have occupied previous linguists. Bloomfield, for example, made intelligibility the criterion for distinguishing between dialects and languages (1933). The first attempts to measure inteligibility were made by American Indianists, headed by C. Voegelin and Z. Harris (1950) and carried into effect by Hickerson and Turner on the Iroquois languages and Pierce on Algonquin (1952). The method was to play taped texts to Indians with similar languages and quantify the transmission of information. Their percentages ran from zero to 75 per cent comprehension, which was held to be a very good understanding. These early experiments suffered from various weaknesses, e.g. that the informants had to know enough Spanish and English to translate into these languages. Also that the translation skill varies greatly among individuals.

It was quickly discovered that other factors than the purely linguistic one played an important part. In a study of two South American tribes by Olmsted (1954), he found that the Achumawis did not understand the Atsuwegis, but the latter did understand the former. Olmsted called this "non-reciprocal intelligibility" and accounted for it by observing that tribe one looked down on tribe two and refused to learn anything from them.

Others who have considered such problems are Ferguson and Gumperz in a monograph (1960) on language varieties in South Asia. They found that there was often a low correlation between linguistic criteria and mutual understanding. They pointed out that extralinguistic factors accounted for the discrepancey. So the use of language features is not enough to distinguish between dialects and standards. Just the very fact that a standard exists is enough to distort the relationship between dialects.

A scholar who long has taken an interest in this kind of situation is the German Heinz Kloss. He began with a survey of the development of Germanic "languages of culture" in 1952, a book that was revised and greatly expanded in an edition of 1978. In these he set up a contrast between what he called *Abstandssprache* and *Ausbausprache,* the former languages that were so far apart as to be obviously unintelligible, while the latter were related languages that were separately developed into standard languages. In Scandinavia

Finnish, Samish, and Greenlandic are obvious examples of the first, while the leading Germanic languages are examples of the second. Actually, Icelandic and Faroese would today have to be reckoned as having developed a good deal of distance. Kloss cites a passage from Bright's experience with the Navahos. When he played one of his tapes for them, they declared that they knew these texts were close to them, but they couldn't quite translate; they were on the verge of understanding. I am sure that this is much the same as other Scandinavians feel about Icelandic and Faroese, or in some cases even about Danish.

Such empirical testing has been carried on for some time in Mexico by the Summer Institute for Linguistics, as reported by Kirk (1970) and Casad (1974). The goal here has been to find out which dialects are similar enough to be comprised under a single standard orthography. These students have wide experience and master statistical methods. Casad has proposed a theory of intelligibility, in which the independent variables are the historical conditions and the socio-economic relations between the groups. He admits that the mathematics is not yet adequate to dispense with informant testing.

Karam (1975) has also developed hypotheses to account for such relationships. The blocking of closely related dialects may be due to the sound systems, the grammar, and the lexicon, or it may be due to language attitudes. In West Africa, according to Hockett (1958: 326-7), they speak of a "two-day" dialect and a "one-week" dialect, according to how long it takes to unravel the system of another dialect. I should describe the relation of Norwegian to Danish as a "two-week" dialect, which was about the time it took for me to communicate easily with the Danes of Copenhagen.

While there is no language called "Scandinavian," there are cases of mutual adjustment of the type that in some parts of the world lead to *koine's, lingua francas,* or even *creole-pidgin.* One can certainly speak of cases of "interlanguage." Maurud recognizes that Norwegians yield to Swedes and freely adopt Swedish expressions in contact siutations.(p. 141) Icelanders have a long tradition of learning Danish as their Nordic contact language. But if you ask an Icelander if he speaks Danish, he will reply that he speaks "Scandinavian." What we hear is Danish with an Icelandic pronunciation, which is not unlike a West Norwegian speaking Bokmål Norwegian. In an attempt to confirm my impression I studied the speech of two Icelanders now living in Boston. Both of these learned Danish in school and came to Denmark at the age of twenty. Their speech lacks the Danish glottal catch and is uncertain about stress placement: either they follow Icelandic practice by placing all stresses on the primary syllable or they hypercorrect: /fyˊsik/ for /fysikˊ/, /påˊståˊ/ for /påˊstå/. The indistinct shwa for *e* is replaced by a clear *e:* *høne* is /høˊne/. One of them has learned to use throat-*r,* but constantly forgets and uses his tongue. Intervocalic geminates are pronounced long: *kunne* /kun:e/. In *ng* the *g* is pronounced: *overtrening(k)*.

These men assured me that no attempt was made in Icelandic schools to teach Danish pronunciation; their teachers consciously taught them a "Scandinavian" pronunciation so they would be understood throughout Scandinavia. Both of them were shocked to come to Denmark and discover how difficult it was to communicate with Danes.

In the Faroes, which has remained under Danish suzerainty, there is a kind of Danish known as *götudanskt* "street Danish", with Faroese pronunciation and a partly Danish vocabulary. Patriotic Faroe islanders try to suppress Danish elements in writing. Hagström has written an article studying the Faroese rendition of Danish (1977; see also Clausén 1978).

It is clear that the dominant Norwegian standard, Bokmål-Norwegian, arose in much the same way, as a Norwegian version of Danish. Four centuries of Danish writing and teaching in school led to the rise of an urban standard that passed from being a pidgin to becoming a creole. The orthographic reforms from 1907 to 1938 allowed this language to assume an outwardly Norwegian form and left it open to further nativization. A result is that the loss of Danish role models has left this language as the most "Scandinavian" of the Nordic idioms. Tests have shown it is the most easily understood by Danes and Swedes. From time to time voices have been raised to make of it a kind of Scandinavian norm.

Danes have generally speaking shown the most enthusiasm for "Nordic" movements; at least in theory they have the most to gain. I have noted marked differences in the intelligibility of Danes, e.g. people from Århus (in Jutland) are easier to understand than Copenhageners. A Danish linguist said to me humorously: "We Danes can easily talk so that you will understand us, but it sounds awful." Actors with precise diction are easier to understand. One friend of mine spoke of a brand of Danish he called "travel guide Danish" or "mid-Sound Danish", a mixture of Danish and Swedish.

Swedes are the ones who show the least interest in adapting their speech to fellow Scandinavians. For a goodly period they have now been the dominant Scandinavian people and as such feel they have little to learn from their neighbors. They take the usual "big-brother" attitude, well-known on the European mainland from the French. Swedes need ear training in relation to Danish and lexical instruction in relation to Norwegian. In spite of all good will on the part of academic Swedes and of Swedish institutions, there is relatively little of genuinely Scandinavian spirit.

The alternative for Scandinavians is to turn to an outside language, formerly German, now English, in their mutual contacts. One regrets this necessity, if that is what it is. In the long run it would mean the death of all the Nordic languages and of the culture they represent.

Chapter 14

English: Modernization

> Loanwords have been called mileposts of
> linguistics, because we can with their help
> date language changes. But they are also
> mileposts of general history, especially
> cultural history, as they show us the course
> of history and often tell us more about
> contacts between peoples than the dry
> accounts in old annals.
>
> Otto Jespersen (1902)

The Scandinavian peoples are well on the way to becoming bilingual, with
English as a second language used in all forms of international communication.
One consequence of this language learning has been a rapid growth in the use
of English terms and turns of phrase in the Scandinavian languages themselves.
After World War II the invasion became so overwhelming that Scandinavian
thinkers became alarmed. Some efforts have been made to stem the tide, to
put one's finger in the dike. An unhappy disaster in the North Sea oil fields
off Norway thrust a new word into the Norwegian language: *blow-out*. A
headline in *Aftenposten* (Oslo) ran: "Eksperter drøfter blow-out bak lukkede
dører" (Experts discuss blowout behind closed doors) (May 24, 1977). In
the text, however, a Norwegian equivalent was used, *utblåsning*, previously
used only for the exhaust phase of a gasoline motor. The headline writer
clearly preferred the shorter and more precise English term, and by this
time his readers were no doubt only too familiar with its meaning.

The example illustrates in an almost frightening way the Scandinavian
dilemma. An industry financed by American capital and employing a
technology developed in English establishes itself off the Scandinavian coast,
where any undertaking is of vital interest to the future of these countries.
It is only the latest in a chain of historical events that have turned English
into an absolutely necessary resource language for Scandinavia. In 1902
Otto Jespersen could list some seventy loanwords that had filtered into
Scandinavian in the nineteenth century. He characterized them as merely
technical terms for "concepts and things that we have learned from the
English." (Jespersen 1902)

They were public institutions like *jury, budget, club*; industrial phenomena
like *strike, lockout, boycott*; high life terms like *gentleman, dandy, snob*;
clothing like *shawl, plaid, smoking* (jacket) "tuxedo"; sports terms like *start,*

handicap, odds; the names of sports like *football, tennis, boxing*; games and inventions like *whist, bicycle, tourist*; railroad words like *tender, wagon, tunnel*; seamen's terms like *dock, cut, schooner*; literary forms like *essay, humor, interview*; and miscellaneous phenomena of modern life like *clown, humbug,* and *reporter.*

Today one cannot walk the streets of a sizable Scandinavian town or open a newspaper without seeing more or less disguised English words. *Flickshopen* is a store in Stockholm, *Daddy's Dance Hall* a nightspot in Copenhagen, *East Side* a clothing store in Oslo (which advertises that it sells *in-wear*, including *matchende jeans.*) Reading random issues for every word in leading Scandinavian newspapers I was struck less by the number of English words than by their conspicuousness. They were often spelled in English and identified objects or ideas being promoted as novel and fascinating. In the lists of "new words" published between 1955 and 1969 the ratio of English-derived words outnumbered those from French and German by twenty to one. In 1956 the Swedish linguist Ljunggren noted that "English has succeeded Latin, German and French as the pattern of [Scandinavian] language and style." He also pointed out that the words borrowed were much the same in the three major languages. (Ljunggren 1956).

More than a half century ago the Swedish writer Louis de Geer attacked the dominance of English, referring to it as "engelska sjukan" (the English sickness, usually meaning "rickets"). In 1962 Dahlstedt wrote that "a world language − the American and European English − is on the point of bursting the dams of the old course of Swedish." In 1960 the Norwegian linguist Hellevik considered the problem of English words of such importance that he called on the Language Commission of Norway to put it on their agenda. Here, he suggested, was a problem on which both Norwegian languages could cooperate. In 1962 the Swedish linguist Ståhle called for Swedes to make use of native resources and to sift carefully the new material. (Dahlstedt et al. 1962: 65-73). More drastically and pessimistically, the Norwegian critic and publisher Groth wrote in 1960: "The small language groups are today in danger of being absorbed by the great. In ten years English may have won hegemony in Iceland, in thirty years in Norway, in fifty years in Sweden." (*Dagbladet*, Aug. 3, 1960). It seems that Scandinavians are looking for someone to cap the apparently irresistible blow-out of English words, a "brønndreper" (well-killer) to cite the Anglo-inspired word.

In view of the importance of the problem, one wonders that relatively little research has been done on it in Scandinavia. Before one can adopt measures to regulate the flow, one needs to know from what sources it stems, and to recognize that the problem is European and global. It has been given close and continuing attention in France and Germany, but in Scandinavia the only book-length monograph is Stene's *English Loan-Words in Modern*

Norwegian, completed in 1939, but delayed by the war from publication until 1945. She called it "a snapshot of a thing in motion" and prophesied that English influence would grow. She called for whoever should describe the new phase of English influence to start work immediately.

So far no one has picked up the gauntlet. Articles and unpublished theses have been written, but have only nibbled at the problem. The very idea of language in motion has not appealed to most linguists, who either wish to study past languages available in texts or present languages that are standardized. Only in recent years have some discovered (or rediscovered) language variation as a challenging problem (Weinreich, Herzog, Labov 1968). It is a central theme in the new discipline of sociolinguistics.

To fill this gap in the literature we will need a comprehensive collection of the English loans and influences in current speech and writing as well as an excerpting of earlier writings. But the job of collecting is a task for Sisyphos and can never be completed, since new words are constantly appearing in response to current needs. It will be necessary to include also the subtler influences on vocabulary and phraseology, on syntax and semantics, even the thought patterns. For we are here dealing with more than the adoption of English *words*: we are dealing with the adoption of English and American *ideas*. This involves the entire function of English in modern life. Why do Scandinavians need to know English?

The basic reason is that English is the chief instrument of *modernization* in the western (and westernized) world. Modernization is a term of wide use, generally favorable or even prestigious in its connotation. Modernizing a house means to improve its plumbing, rearrange its rooms for more comfortable living, redecorating it according to the latest fashions. There is great emphasis in our culture on being up to the moment, in ideas, art, music, politics, food, clothing, and entertainment. Advertisers lay stress on being "modern," no doubt reflecting in their own interest a common ambition among their customers. Unfortunately it is a fleeting achievement, for what is modern today is old hat tomorrow. To stay "modern" a language has to remain in constant flux. Ferguson has defined modernization in language as making it fully translatable for the terminology of technological, social, artistic, and intellectual endeavor in our time (Ferguson 1971). A fully developed language must have words for "atom" and "nuclear power," as well as for "social security," "proletariat," "birth control," "rock and roll music", and "existentialism." Such terms must have precise equivalents, so that books, articles, radio and TV programs may be transferable from one language to another without loss of information. At the same time each language must maintain its own native tradition of creative writing, which may resist modernization by virtue of the emotional values associated with traditional life. Poetry and artistic prose are notoriously difficult to translate, and any attempt to make this part of the language translatable would threaten it with sterility and loss of intimacy.

A century ago Scandinavians did not feel compelled to learn English, aside from sailors and merchants. Ibsen, Strindberg, and Kierkegaard knew little or no English. Only in 1850 and 1857 did Danish and Norwegian higher schools, respectively, introduce the teaching of English, and similar dates no doubt apply in Sweden (Bang 1962: 31; Stene 1945; 143). Today English is the most widely taught language in Scandinavia. It is the chief window to the innovations of the modern world, the language "of wider communication", which permits the free exchange of information in an increasingly complex and interrelated world. (Haugen 1976a: 63-72)

It is a truism of bilingual research, as observed earlier in this book, that when any considerable number of persons become bilingual, they find difficulty in keeping their two languages apart. A reason is quite simply that each language is an arbitrary and only partly motivated set of signs. It is a purely historical accident that the English verb *to stick* has a different range of meanings from its Scandinavian cognate *sticka/stikke*. The bilingual who naturally identifies two so similar words will be misled into saying "I have to stick" when s/he means "I have to leave" (one of its Scandinavian meanings). Conversely, s/he can be misled into saying in Scandinavian "jag måste sticka till det/jeg må stikke til det" when s/he means "I have to stick to it," this not being one of its Scandinavian meanings. Such overlappings, sometimes known as "false friends" (after French *faux amis*), are only part of the problem.

In learning another language, the learner always discovers gaps in his own. Each language is like a map of the reality its users perceive, and just as different maps of the same terrain may convey different information, so different languages draw a different set of distinctions in the real world. Each new word learned identifies one of the guideposts in the world of its speakers, as we shall see in a later chapter. Along with the word come new associations that bring it readily to mind, and the learner finds it useful to adopt the word in order to enrich his/her thinking.

An ideal bilingual would keep the two maps of reality apart, but this requires an almost schizophrenic living in two worlds: I have called it a case of *schizoglossia*. The effects of bilingual merger are well-known among immigrants in the United States. Under the pressure of the dominant English they have to learn, it becomes natural and normal for them to adopt numerous English words, even beyond what is by some considered "necessary." They adopt words like "field," "street," and "fence," even though they had words at home for all of these. English becomes their new source for innovation in language, because its words fit the map of reality within whose framework they now live. Intellectual leaders among the emigrants have labored without avail to keep the old mother tongue pure.

When they discover that their countrymen back "home" are undergoing a similar influence, they may become discouraged and resentful. A Norwegian-American editor I knew expressed annoyance at reading in Norwegian newspapers that an airplane had "krasjet" (crashed) instead of "styrtet ned" (fallen down).

One can take either a *puristic* or a *pragmatic* attitude to such innovations. Purism is closely connected with national feeling and has blossomed in periods of patriotic fervor. In the nineteenth century the Swedish author Viktor Rydberg and the Norwegian pedagogue Knud Knudsen proclaimed the need of purifying their languages of "foreign" slag. Pragmatic thinking is more likely to prevail under the pressures of communication. Speakers who are conversing with other bilinguals do not wish to interrupt their train of thought to find a different word for some foreign concept. Journalists who have to meet deadlines will take the word they find in their sources rather than search their minds for a native substitute. Loanwords like *tape* and *teenager* may be replaced by loan creations like *ljudband/lydbånd* or *tonåring/tenåring*, but they tend to persist; the result in either case is a borrowing.

The decision on how to clothe the new idea is an internal matter for each language. As is well-known, Icelandic, partly followed by Faroese, has insisted on maintaining a puristic tradition in the hope of staving off the kind of structural alterations that the mainland languages underwent in the Middle Ages.

English is itself a striking instance of language pragmatism: like the English people it is a complex mixture of disparate elements that have been at least in part harmonized into a functional whole. The Germanic base brought to England by the Anglo-Saxons has been reduced to an almost creolized set of form words in a more analytic than synthetic grammar. The lexicon reflects the successive ruling elites of England from the Romans and Celts to the Vikings and the Normans. By natural selection it has achieved a form that meets the needs of an international language better than any of its artifical rivals like Esperanto.

The translators of English are often troubled by the English freedom to draw both on the underworld of slang and popular entertainment and on the classical Latin and Greek vocabulary. They tend to adopt the popular words whole and to unduly latinize the academic style, as shown in the following excerpt from a newspaper article on psychiatry:

"Nettverksterapi, forebyggende arbeid, konsultasjon, familieterapi, poliklinisk behandling osv. er in − miljøterapi med vekt på trygghet, struktur og grensesetting innenfor rammen av en institusjonsavdeling er *ikke* in." (Network therapy, preventative effort, consultation, family therapy, polyclinical treatment etc. is in − environmental therapy with emphasis on security, structure, and borderlines within the frame of an institutional division is *not* in.) (*Dagbladet* June 11, 1976).

This mixture of slang ("in") and technical jargon is also characteristic of Swedish. Tingbjörn reports some of the Anglo-Latinisms found among sports writers: *sitt dubiösa anseende* "his dubious reputation", *notoriskt svag* "notoriously weak." (Tingbjörn 1976). English has here tended to create pedagogical problems in the ongoing trend toward democratizing the Scandinavian languages, as discussed by Molde (1976).

At the same time English has added nuances to the languages. *Service* corresponds to *tjänst/tjeneste*, and it is borrowed only in the sense of service offered by such modern institutions as oil stations, repair shops, and hotels. *Sex* means the same as *kön/kjønn/køn*, but is borrowed primarily in reference to its commercialized and pornographic forms. *Juice* translates Scandinavian *saft*, but with the development of refrigeration and commercially prepared juices, the word is now normal for the latter: *eplesaft* is now canned apple juice, while *eplejuice* is raw apple juice. *Weekends* were formerly known as *helg* 'holiday', but with the secular weekend one can hardly use it, e.g. *litt løssluppen weekend-stemning* (a bit of merry weekend mood). A *bag* is larger and roomier than a *handväska/håndveske/håndtaske* and it is more suitable for modern shopping at the *shopping center* (or *butikcentrum/kjøpesenter*, as they are coming to be known)

Once English words have been borrowed and thoroughly adapted, they go on to live their lives as Scandinavian citizens, albeit naturalized. Old loans like *job, mob*, and *snob* have spawned verbs with new meanings: *jobba/jobbe* "work", *mobba/mobbe* "bully", *snobba/snobbe* "put down".

English has also become a prolific source of clichés and standing phrases, often for humorous or nonchalant effects: "mennesker som fightet for at vi skulle få friheten igjen" (people who fought so that we should get our freedom back, *Dagbladet* May 14, 1977, p. 4), "Is-prinsessen herself" (the ice-princess herself, *Dagbladet* Nov. 18, 1960). These seem to be more than instrumental loans: they border on integrative motivation, i.e. a desire to identify oneself with the international scene.

The problem of orthographic adaptation is still a topic of animated discussion. Old loans have generally been adapted, e.g. *gäng/gjeng* "gang", *klubb* "club", *kutta/kutte* "cut", while recent loans vacillate, e.g. *tape* is now *tejp* in Swedish, *teip/tape* in Norwegian, *tape* in Danish (following a typical pattern). A happy innovation was the launching in Swedish by linguist Ture Johannisson of *plast* as a word for "plastics"; this has spread throughout Scandinavia.

There is some awareness of the French and German discussion of these problems, but one difference is that for them it is a matter of stylistic purity. But in Scandinavia one also encounters fears that English may lead to extinction of the native languages. It is my conviction that this is unlikely; we know of no such example. But it would be well if the Scandinavians showed more pride and less resignation in the face of English influences on the mass media. English brings great advances, but modernity can be bought at too high a price. The words of the thirteenth century author of the *King's Mirror* are still valid: Learn foreign languages, but do not neglect your own!

Chapter 15

Faroese: Ecology

One of the smallest language communities in the world is located in the North Atlantic, about three hundred miles north of Scotland's Shetland Islands and midway between Iceland and the west coast of Norway. Here, on eighteen habitable islands, buffeted by winter storms, the Faroe Islanders have lived continuously for more than a thousand years, ever since their ancestors sailed out from Norway and occupied the islands. On land their chief occupation is raising sheep, after which the islands are (presumably) named, as well as birding on the incredible bird cliffs. But mostly they make their living from the sea, fishing and whaling. They live in small seacoast villages, each one tightly knit, and often isolated from its neighbors much of the year. According to the census of 1969 they number only about 38,000, of whom some 10,000 live in the capital, Tórshavn.

They are one remnant of what was once Norway's North Atlantic empire, including the islands off the Scottish coast, Iceland, Greenland, and parts of Ireland and Scotland. Today they are under the rule of Denmark, as they have been since Norway and Denmark were united in the late fourteenth century. But in 1948 they achieved home rule under the Danish king. The Danes mostly take it for granted that they are Danish and speak a peculiar kind of Danish. In some handbooks one will find it stated that they speak a dialect of Icelandic. Both of these opinions are mistaken, as any Faroe Islander will be glad to inform you. My own private inclination is to regard their language as a kind of Norwegian! But even this turns out to be wrong.

What do they speak and write, and what are the problems that face them in their social and literary life? How can their problems of communication tell us something about the life of a language and illustrate some general principles of what I have found it useful to call *language ecology?*

Ecology, according to Webster, "is concerned with the interrelationship of organisms and their environments." If we substitute "languages" for environments in this definition, we get a very acceptable definition of language ecology. Languages have in common with organisms their persistence through time and their more or less gradual change, but they are not inherited biologically. While organisms pass their features on through the genes, languages pass them on through the brain. A language lives only as long as someone learns it and uses it and teaches it to someone else. Language is not part of man's biological heritage, though the capacity for language certainly is. But individual languages *are* part of his societal heritage. Language ecology is therefore societal, and should form a significant part of a complete science of sociology.

The model that most people have in mind when thinking about language and society is the uniform or monodialectal community. In such a community everyone speaks the same dialect, though of course with individual variations. But these do not identify the speaker as belonging to any other group. This comes closest to N. Chomsky's much cited definition of "a completely homogeneous speech-community." (Chomsky 1965) In a pure form no such community exists, and the definition is useful only for a mathematical-logical theory of language.

In most real communities there are people who at least passively know some other dialect or variety of the common language. There is one kind of what we may call "bidialectalism" that has been identified by sociolinguists as *diglossia,* first defined by Ferguson and developed by Fishman. Ferguson identified as his best examples the situation in Greece, with its formal, religious or official writing known as Katharevousa, which contrasts with its popular, literary form known as Demotike. He called the former "high" (H), the latter "low" (L), and identified similar situations in Arabic, with Classical vs. Popular; in German Switzerland, with High German vs. Swiss German; in Haiti, with standard French vs. Haitian Creole. While Ferguson limited his cases to closely related languages, Fishman extended diglossia to include cases in which two languages performed distinct functions in the same society, e.g. Hebrew and Yiddish in Israel (or better: in pre-war Russia).

A third ecological situation is that of a truly bilingual society. In its pure form this would be one in which two distinct but nationally united groups each maintained its language and communicated through bilingual interpreters. Belgium, Canada, and Switzerland spring to mind as examples. The number of bilinguals will depend on the degree of interaction between the groups. Shopkeepers in Montreal have a keen eye for the appearance of their customers and can often tell which language to use before the speaker even opens his mouth. The distinction between the languages is more one of speech partners than it is of functions.

We may call our three types of societies *homogeneous, diglossic,* and *bilingual,* or more economically, A, B, and C.

These differences condition different processes of acquisition, development, and maintenance. In A everyone learns virtually the same language and passes it on to his descendants. In B everyone learns the L language while some also learn the H language, creating status differences within the group. In C children learn both languages and can communicate to both groups, or they learn only one and form a monolingual group within the whole.

In A changes will occur as they are needed. In B a gradual osmosis may occur between the H and L language, mostly from H to L, but possibly also the other way. These will appear as "interferences", often called loans, which may or may not become a permanent part of both. In C the amount of interference will be determined by the relative status and the amount of interaction between the languages.

Maintenance is no problem in A: as long as the population remains, its language will go on. In B there may also be great stability, but elements of change are present. If roles in the elite are opened to everyone, as when a universal school system is established, either the H or the L language will win out (as English did over French). Society C may result, with various groups claiming new rights for their own languages. C is often an unstable society, resulting from migrations, dislocations, wars, or revolutions. One can predict that B will become C or attempt to return to A.

This progression from A through B to C has raised many problems, among them some especially acute ones in the formerly colonial nations now emerging in Africa and Asia. One measure that nations have found helpful at certain stages is to enter upon a program of *language planning*. This amounts to a deliberate interference with the ecology on behalf of the group involved. The goal is to create a *standardized* form of the language, which will then be taught to the growing members of the community.

In its early centuries the Faroe Islands were a typical community A, in which its native dialects developed away from Old Norse and gradually split apart. The lack of a written tradition permitted speakers to deviate unconsciously from the old.

But with the establishment of the Lutheran church and a trade monopoly from Denmark, the writing of Danish was introduced and a small number of Danish speakers formed an economic and social elite. In this respect the Faroes were treated no differently from Norway, Iceland, or provincial Denmark itself. All folk speech was a low prestige language, with Danish in a diglossic relation that gave it high prestige. Among the population Faroese continued to be spoken, but a creolized Danish (known as *götu-dönsk* "street Danish") was used in communicating with the Danish officials, who rarely bothered to learn the local speech. In the course of time some of this creolized Danish influenced the Faroese of the natives, giving it a heavy infusion of Danish words and constructions. There was imminent danger of the complete death of Faroese, like that of the Irish, and this might indeed have happened if access to Denmark had been as easy for the Faroese as England was for the Irish. But remoteness gave the Faroese time to develop a countermovement on behalf of their language before it was too late (Haugen 1968).

The first preserved attempt to write modern Faroese was made in 1773 by a 27-year old student at the University of Copenhagen, a native of the Faroes named Jens Christian Svabo. Svabo's life story is the pathetic one of a swallow who never made a summer. But he did a fantastic job, which was recognized only long after his death. He rescued for posterity the texts of numerous medieval dance ballads which are the chief glory of traditional Faroese literature. He wrote a remarkable ethnographic study of the islands, and he collected many thousands of Faroese words which form the basis of its modern dictionary. It is hard to conceive that anyone could have tried to make a standard language of Faroese without his work. But he himself did not have any such ambitions. He recognized the possibility, and he pointed the way, by noting (in 1773) that if anyone should want to restore it as a language, he would have to bring it back to "its pristine purity" by restoring the lost Old Norse words, eradicating the new and "corrupted" Danish words, and giving the language, "if not a new pronunciation, in any case a new orthography." In the terms of his time, this was in fact a program of language planning.

But in spite of his love of the language, he was too much of an eighteenth-century rationalist to propose anything so impractical and arduous. Instead he suggested that it would be much more sensible to work for introducing Danish and teaching everyone to use it correctly (Djupedal 1964).

This was certainly the policy of the Danish government. Faroese youngsters like Svabo, who showed promise, were educated in Danish. But at home they continued to talk Faroese and to sing (and dance) their ballads in that language. During the early years of the nineteenth century a new nationalistic wind blew through Europe, as we have seen, and a few Danish and Faroese students of language began to cultivate the writing of Faroese. The famous Danish linguist Rasmus Rask wrote its first scientific grammar in 1811. In 1823 a Faroese pastor translated the Gospel according to St. Matthew, and in 1832 the Old Icelandic saga of the Faroe Islands.

But the crucial threshold was passed in 1846 when Svabo's nephew, the Reverend V. U. Hammershaimb, devised a new etymologizing orthography, just what Svabo had said would be needed if Faroese were to be brought back to its "pristine purity." This spelling saddled the children of the Faroes for all time with a learning problem similar to that faced by English and American children. The spelling does not reflect the pronunciation directly, as Svabo's had done, but through the intermediary of its history and its grammar.

The effect is to keep the written images of words and morphemes constant, even when the pronunciation changes. Just as we in English spell the plural suffix -*s* whether it is pronounced /s/ or /z/, so in Faroese the Old Norse letter ð (which was pronounced as *th* in *this*) is now spoken as /j/ or /v/ or not at all. This makes it possible to spell the language so that it looks like a "dialect" of Icelandic, although they are actually very far apart and hardly intelligible when spoken. The written form is therefore easy to read, but hard to write. It covers over the discrepancies of its dialects, and it is dignified and traditional, as an orthography probably should be.

After a century of efforts to develop Faroese into a standard language, it did become the main language taught in the public schools when home rule was granted in 1948. In slow motion it had gone through the four steps I have named above as part of the planning process: selection, codification (by Hammershaimb), implementation, and elaboration.

We may well ask: was it worth it? On this there may well be differing opinions, just as people can differ on problems of natural ecology. The existence of a Faroese language with a burgeoning literature is today a fact. But a population of less than forty thousand islanders is at the mercy of a world in which they cannot live without contact with other languages. Danish continues to be the chief foreign language taught and is for many Faroese still the most natural language to write. Spoken Faroese is far from having given up the Danish words the islanders are taught to avoid in writing. The islanders have deliberately moved themselves into a society C in their efforts to become a society A. In official work they are often confused and uncertain as to which language to use and exactly how to handle it. Formerly, as in any society B, the prestige was clearly on the side of the high-status language, here Danish, but few could speak it. Today Faroese competes with Danish and often comes off badly because of inadequate resources. Danish is rejected as a symbol of domination, but has become much better known because of the rapid urbanization of life through modern communications. It is typical that while there is a not inconsiderable literature in Faroese, the best (and best-known) Faroese writer, William Heinesen, writes in Danish.

If we estalbish *status* and *intimacy* as the two dimensions of the roles played by competing languages in a community, the low-status language in a diglossic situation is usually also a high-intimacy language. In medieval France Latin was high in status but low in intimacy, while French was the reverse; in Norman England, English had low status, but high intimacy. When a traditional society gives way to one with high mobility, as in modern life, the roles are upset. In the Faroes the Danish environment has shrunk to insignificance, but the role of Danish as a medium of contact with outside culture has not been reduced. As a student of mine who has worked in the Faroes once wrote me: the young people no longer think Danish is elegant, only that it is more exciting. "In an ecological sense, the influence of Danish here is felt at a more basic level." There is a good deal of irritation about expressions that are used in written Faroese and are felt to be "invented" and "unnatural," usually imitations of Icelandic words.

Most people still think of Faroese as something you talk, and they don't like it if they have to look up a word in the dictionary. The movement to purify the language has made people conscious of Danicisms in their speech, but has not caused them to eliminate them if they still feel them as natural. This is obviously a problem in the creation of a literary style. The most successful written Faroese is that which deals directly with Faroese conditions or similar ones elsewhere. The general knowledge of Danish weakens the motivation for developing the literary language beyond this traditional base.

A few words to sum up the "balance sheet" of language ecology. It is impossible to answer with any assurance the question of whether it is "worthwhile." Americans are impatient with groups that claim rights for their own language. But the steamroller approach to small languages has much in common with the superhighway that flattens and destroys our landscape. What is group cohesion and ethnic pride worth? How can one measure in money the values that are lost when a group gives up its language in favor of another?

The Faroese are fond of pointing out to visitors that since 1900 their population has doubled and their standard of living has multiplied. The neighboring English-speaking Shetland Islands have lost half their population and are being wiped out economically. They are more than willing to let you think that their fierce insistence on being themselves has had something to do with it. They may be right. It needs to be considered when we study the ecology of language.

Chapter 16

Icelandic: Pronominal Address

It is refreshing now and then to be reminded that even Icelandic has changed from that Norwegian which the settlers brought with them in the ninth century, and that it is not, in the words of one writer, "eine versteinerte Sprachform" (an ossified language form) (Décsy 1973: 48). One striking change involving phonological, morphological, syntactic, and sociolinguistic problems is that of the dual and plural pronouns of the first and second persons. Succinctly stated: ON *vit* "we" dual and *þit* "you" dual have become *við* "we" plural and *þið* "you" plural, while ON *vér* "we" plural and *þér* "you" plural have become "we" and "you" honorific.

This change was the theme of a doctoral dissertation at the University of Reykjavík in 1972 by Helgi Guðmundsson. He assigned the Icelandic change to the 17th century and attributed the loss of the dual to the rise of the honorific.

To some the problem may seem a small one, but I believe it illustrates in microcosm some of the major interests of linguistics in the past hundred and fifty years, and that it is worthy of attention.

In his "Introduction" the author has set himself the task of providing a theoretical background for the use of the dual. Like so much else in lingustics, the study of the dual goes back to Wilhelm von Humboldt, who in 1827 became the first to call attention to its extraordinary linguistic interest (Humboldt 1963). From having been thought of as an oddity of Greek or at best Indo-European grammar, it was now realized that the dual is or has been a category in the most diverse languages around the world.

To most of us the dual is a puzzling category, since we think of "two" as merely a digit between "one" and "three." But as Humboldt pointed out, the dual reflects a dualistic world view "in dem Satz und Gegensatz" (Humboldt 1963: 137). Hammerich, writing about Eskimo, pointed out that it was not so much "Zweizahl als Paarzahl". His Eskimos were not so much interested in how many there were, but rather whether they occurred in pairs (Hammerich 1959: 17). The dual has two chief roots in human experience: (1) the symmetry of the human body and its limbs; (2) the duality of many human (and animal) relationships, including that of speaker and hearer.

Brugmann (1911: 446) made the additional observation that the dual applied to pairing as such, while the plural left it unspecified. In Prague

School terminology, the plural is unmarked in relation to the dual (Jakobson 1964; Greenberg 1966: 76). Hence the plural may be used for the dual when the two merge or overlap and is likely to be more frequent.

The question of whether the dual is a "primitive" feature may be an idle will-o'-the-wisp, as Guðmundsson maintains (p. 94), but it may be worth considering, since many distinguished linguists have used it to explain the disappearance of the dual. Now that Watkins (1969) has shown that it was probably not an Indo-European category, we should rather ask why it has apparently been revived from time to time. If Germanic *wit and *jut (> *jit) have their *t* from the word for "two," then these are simply pronominal phrases that have been worn down to monosyllables. Tesnière (1925: 262) found that Slovenian and Lithuanian reinforced the old duals by adding "two". If the dual is indeed a marked form of the plural, then the loss of the dual is rather just a change from an obligatory to an optional category.

Contrary to Jespersen (1924: 206), Humboldt admired and appreciated the dual as he knew it in Greek, because it "promoted the philosophical elaboration of understanding." (Humboldt 1963: 143) But a more pragmatic writer like Pater Schmidt associated it with nomadic cattle-raising cultures (Schmidt 1926: 326). Wackernagel (1950-7: 1.77) attributed its loss in Greek to the rapid cultural development of the Greeks in Asia Minor. These contradictory and obviously subjective views have only this core in common: that the absorption of the dual by the plural occurred first among peoples who were in lively contact with their neighbors through trade and conquest.

That Iceland was one of the last countries in Europe to give up the dual is therefore not so much a mark of inferior civilization, as of the lack of urban centers in the Middle Ages. Tesnière went to Slovenia to study the dual because he had learned from Meillet and Cuny that it was "strikingly anachronistic to see an intelligent and civilized people employing in the full twentieth century a category that passes as an index of a retarded civilization." (Tesnière 1925: ix). He did find that the Slovenes were often quite confused about the use of the dual. Hammerich also found that Eskimos in contact with Europeans had reduced their use of the dual (1959: 16).

In fact, the dual is not lost. It has just been transformed, at least in Indo-European, from being an obligatory morphological category in nouns (and by congruence in verbs) to paradigmatic status in the pronouns and then to a completely lexical status in modern Germanic. We still distinguish "one — both — all". We cannot say "all his eyes are blue" nor "all his brothers are older" without implying that there are more than two. There are a number of such words, including *pair, couple, deuce, parents, twins*, which have dual meaning. There are conjunctions like *either* and *whether*, as well as the comparative of the adjective, which imply two members. In Icelandic there are words like *feðgar* "father and son" and *mæðgur* "mother and daughter."

There is no such thing as an indispensible morphological category: even such forms as tense, gender, number, or person can be expressed otherwise than by suffixes. The Indo-European languages show a trend towards the replacement of suffixes by form words, but it is neither inevitable nor irreversible, as is shown by the growth of such forms as the suffixed definite article and reflexive verbs in Scandinavian. To say that the loss of the dual is a transition from "concrete" to "asbstract" thinking is hardly adequate (Gauthiot 1912). As the system of numbers became more important in a trading culture, one may suppose that the dual as marker of coupling lost significance.

In his chapter 3 Guðmundsson embarks on a fullscale study of the semantic category of number in the pronouns. He commendably keeps the entire system before us and shows it changing as a whole. He sets up a series of six stages as models to account for the entire development. Even in the earliest datable texts we have, the skaldic poems, there are instances of the use of the plural to refer to single persons. While our author is inclined to be dubious about the origins of this usage, whether it is early poetic style or due to outside influence, I am inclined to suspect the latter.

The appeal to the individual of making use of the plural is in part due to its ambiguity: it is not really a plural unless he is speaking on behalf of a collectivity. It may involve anything from modesty and evasion of responsibility to self-assertion and assumption of responsibility. The fact that we are not offered any examples from Eddic poetry or from Old English or Old High German poetry makes the idea of a native poetic tradition questionable. From the time of King Ólafr there was French influence at the court, and the development of French *courtoisie* is fulfilled at the court of Hákon Hákonsson, where the *King's Mirror* was written.

The study of honorific pronouns has a long history. If I miss anything in Guðmundsson's account, it is a greater perception of the social dimension. He is familiar with Brown and Gilman's study of "The Pronouns of Power and Solidarity" (Brown and Gilman 1960: 253). In a later study they have replaced these terms with "status" and "intimacy" (Brown and Ford 1961). The seventeenth century was a period of economic and political hardship in Iceland. Danish rule was particularly harsh. A hierarchical society was established that corresponded to that which the rest of Europe had developed by the end of the Middle Ages. In 1655 Thomas Fuller, court chaplain to King Charles II, condemned Quaker usage as "clownishness." (Finkenstaedt 1963: 203)

A puzzling aspect of usage in Guðmundsson's stage 3 (the sagas) is the apparently unmotivated shifting between singular and plural. Subjects speaking to kings switch from *þér* to *þú* even within one sentence. It seems that once the addressee's status has been established, the speaker is free to revert to the unmarked pronoun. Maintenance of a marked pronoun is a redundancy that requires severe social training, which is possible only in a class-divided society.

The author presents an impressive array of texts from the period he regards as crucial for the change, i.e. 1525-1733. Just as there must have been periods and communities where the phonetic realizations of neighboring phonemes overlapped, so he tries to show that in the seventeenth century the honorific and dual meanings coexisted. He finds that the change, beginning in the South around 1600 with the nominative of the first person (*við*), spread over three generations until it was completed around 1700.

Guðmundsson tackles the problem of causation by referring to the ambiguity that resulted. I doubt that this is adequate, since pronominal ambiguity is widespread, cf. English *you*, French *vous*, German *Sie*, and Dano-Norwegian *De*. Recent work by Weinreich, Labov and Herzog (1968) has shown that important factors are the rise of random variation and the ordering of social selection. There must have been something special about the Iceland of the seventeenth century to make *vér* and *þér* inappropriate as plurals except in honorific usage. This was the first century in which Icelanders also became literate in Danish. The Danish *vi* and *I* would seem more dignified and elevated because they were used by and to the rulers of the country, and the practice could easily be transferred to native usage by a simple semantic shift. The Icelanders were already prepared for it by the old courtly usage of the plural, leaving the already ambiguous dual forms to develop into plurals.

There is nothing surprising in such a development, since the whole custom of honorific usage is known to have spread via bilinguals from Rome northwards. Finkenstaedt (1963) has shown how the honorific use of *you* in English arose among bilingual Anglo-Normans, who simply transferred their own use of *vous* into the dominated language. The new rule that entered Icelandic in this century was a kind of concord that required the use of honorifics consistently to certain persons, even when they were not exercising their power.

Guðmundsson extends his net to include parallels to the Icelandic development from the spoken dialects of German, Swedish, Norwegian, and Faroese. In each of these the advancing honorific caught up with the dying dual in time to keep it alive as a plural. The six cases adduced are earlier than Icelandic, and the demonstration of similar results make them almost a Q. E. D. for the author.

The practices described in his Stages 1-3 were also Norwegian, exported to Iceland at the time of the settlement. But by 1350 Norwegian had not only added a *þ* from the verb endings of the second persons (*it, ér > þit, þér*), but an *m* in the first person (*mit, mér*), reflected in the widespread *me* of today. This fourteenth-century system included a dual which took over plural meanings by 1400, which could then be used as honorifics. The system showed its sensitivity to social influence by accepting after 1400 the fashionable forms *vi* and *I* from Danish and Swedish (Tylden 1944). Rather than directly borrowed from written Danish, as Tylden thinks, their present-day domain points rather to urban influence issuing from centers like Oslo, Bergen, and Trondheim into the surrounding countryside. The fourteenth century in Norway was a period when (as Edvard Bull put it), the feudal lords "constantly gain greater power upwards, in relation to the king, and downwards, in relation to the people". A new urban middle class, "the lower nobility", came into being (Bull 1968: 116). For the Norwegian people it was also a period of economic disaster following the Black Death, the entry of the Hanseatic League, and preparation for absorption by the Swedish and eventually the Danish kingdom.

In summing up the results of our investigation of Helgi Guðmundsson's research, I have found the topic of great value as a parade example of linguistic change. In spite of a few critical remarks, I have learned a great deal in working my way through his thesis. He has shown distinct mastery of his material and close familiarity with the linguistic problems involved. He has not done full justice to the sociological and historical settings of the change he has described. Given the gradual disappearance of the dual in an advanced, sophisticated society, he has shown good reason for the particular solution adopted in Icelandic and other Germanic dialects. The overlap of the receding dual with the advancing honorific, influenced by the intrusion of Danish, resulted in the assignment of a new meaning to the dual and the isolation of the honorific.

Chapter 17

Norwegian: Forms of Address

Two provocative articles by Roger Brown and asociates (1960, 1961) showed that forms of address in Europe and America reflected social determinants which they summed up under the two dimensions of *solidarity* ("intimacy") vs. *status* ("power").

In continental European languages these found expression in the choice of pronouns, informal *tu* (*t*) vs. formal *vous* (*v*), while in America (the formal pronoun having displaced *thou*) a similar distinction is expressed by first name (*F*) vs. title (*T*) plus last name (*L*). Brown and Gilman pointed out that in modern usage the formal address variants generally reflected non-solidarity (i.e. social distance) rather than power relations.

In modern Norwegian (as in Swedish; cf. Paulston 1975) the younger generation has gone even farther by abandoning the *v*-pronoun entirely, to the dismay of the older generation. This change in the social meaning of the *t*-pronoun reflects populistic and democratic thinking, which rejects even that mild form of social inequality by which polite society has set itself off from the common man through its use of the *v*-pronoun. The new trend is reflected and even encouraged by the state TV system, which has established the *t*-pronoun as normal in all interviews, from the prime minister down (but not including the king) (*Dagbladet* March 12, 1977).

In Norwegian the informal *t*-pronoun is *du*, objective *deg*, possessive *din* (*ditt, dine*). The formal *v*-pronoun is *De* (pronounced /di/), objective *Dem*, possessive *Deres* (identical except for capitalization with *de* "they", *dem* "them", *deres* "their(s)").

The Norwegian author Johan Borgen (b. 1902) is a sensitive observer of the social scene, acutely conscious of the psychological value of words. He is a speaker and writer of the elite form of Bokmål-Norwegian known in his language as *riksmål*. In a novel entitled *Min arm min tarm* 1972 ("My arm my guts") he has furnished vivid dialogue that is virtually a textbook example of the human relations expressed in forms of address. Borgen is a member of the upper bourgeoisie, but an intellectual rebel against many of its values. He is in an excellent position to show the intertwining of status and solidarity in the life of a Norwegian intellectual. We shall recount the major experiences of his hero in the first twenty pages of the novel and then analyze the role relations involved and their significance for the hero.

Frank Vegårdshei is a *lektor* (teacher) at an Oslo *gymnasium* (junior college). He is a graduate of the Sorbonne and a specialist on French grammar. He comes of a lower-class family and is highly conscious of his own success in transcending its social barriers. But he has remained socially and psychologically insecure. He is self-centered, resentful, easily roused to vengeance for minor slights, indecisive, and more concerned with words than with things.

We meet him in a circumscribed setting, a hospital ward, where he is cast in the role of a patient. He is just coming out of a coma after an ulcer operation when the novel opens. We observe him interacting with the nurse, then with the doctor, then with two fellow patients, and continually with his own inner self, which reminisces about earlier social encounters.

The nurse begins by addressing him by first name and *v*-pronoun: "Frank! Frank! De må våkne nå!" (Frank, Frank, you must wake up now!). As he begins to come out of the coma, she uses the formal title *herr* and *L*(ast name): "Herr Vegårdshei?" (Mr. V.?). A moment later she addresses him by *v*-pronoun and *L* alone; then she alternates between *F* and *L*, calling him "Frank" while introducing herself with *T* and *F* as "søster Else" (sister Else). In her efforts to rouse him she shows complete confusion by treating him alternately as a child and an adult: "Du er ikke ute og kjører nå, Frank. Hører De?" (You're not out driving now, Frank. Do you hear?).

In the doctor's presence she adopts the polite forms *v* and *L*, but the doctor advises her to use *t* and *F*: "Bruk fornavn, si du" (Use the first name, say "du"). On occasion both nurse and doctor address Frank in the first person plural (*n p* for *nous* plural, "we"): "Fint Frank, kom nå så våkner vi" (Fine, Frank, come now, let's awake); "Nå, Vegårdshei, har vi sloppet luften?" (Well, V., have we let the air out?). By including themselves in the address, they have expressed a touch of sympathy, in a style reminiscent of the nursery.

In Frank's first state of confusion he takes her for the doctor and uses *v*; when she corrects his error, he adopts *t* and becomes loving: "Du har reddet mitt liv, jeg elsker deg" (You have saved my life, I love you). He seems to think she is his estranged wife, Kamma.

When the doctor comes, Frank takes him to be his colonel from his life as a recruit and greets him with his professional title, prefaced by the formal *herr*: "Herr oberst" (Mr. Colonel). He reports with his identification number and *L*: "86 18 02 Vegårdshei." As his confusion clears, he returns to the socially correct distance marker, *v L* to the doctor, *v T₂ F* to the nurses. But in moments of stress he reverts to markers of his lower-class origin, protesting to the nurse that "hele magan kommer til å dette ut på meg" (the whole tummy is going to fall out on me). The nurse pretends to be shocked to hear such forms as *magan* for correct *maven* and gently chides him, reminding him of his social status: "Hvordan er det De snakker, Vegårdshei, lektor og alt og så magan." (How are you talking, V., teacher and all, and then 'magan').

Meanwhile we have shared some of his internal dialog, beginning with a nightmare of French grammatical forms, "endless columns of subjunctives, all kinds of cases," "storming soundlessly toward him without mercy." Painful episodes recall his linguistic problems at the French lycée in Rouen and the Sorbonne in Paris. His name was held to be unpronounceable, coming out something like Vegæi, and his first name was confusingly like that of "the coin they all have too little of." Flashbacks occur from an old collision with a Swedish car, a collision that led to his unhappy marriage.

Once he is ambulatory, he becomes aware of his companions, in beds number 1 and 2. He decides, thinking of himself as "en godlynt person bak alle sine stengsler" (a well-meaning person behind all his barriers), to introduce himself to them in "full utrustning" (full panoply). This means *F L* plus age, title, and illness: "Frank Vegårdshei, 32, lektor, magesår" (F. V., 32, teacher, ulcer). The replies reveal their social status as members of the folk. No. 1 merely gives *L*, age, and illness: "Aslaksen, 77, prostata". No. 2 gives no age, only *L* and *T*: "Olsen her, stuert, levera" (Olsen here, steward, the liver).

After no. 1 Frank is uncomfortable at his use of title, fearing that he has sounded snobbish. But no. 2 proves to be a hearty, unselfconscious son of the people, who speaks lower-class Oslo (*levera, bena* "the liver, the feet") and expresses his wish for a bottle of wine (which his liver condition strictly prevents). He naturally uses *t* and later develops a friendly nickname (*N*), a shortening (Vegår) based on Frank's *L*. When Frank responds with *t L*, Olsen asks him to use *F*: "Kall meg Tom".

Frank finds it difficult to establish such immediate intimacy, especially as it involves him in Tom's plot to secure that forbidden bottle of wine. Frank reacts with a combination of repulsion and fascination at Tom's "vulgarity." Tom does not hesitate to use a word like "pisse," where Frank even in his thoughts uses the euphemistic term "vannlating" (letting of water). He thinks, "Hvorfor ikke si pisse når det heter pisse, hvorfor ikke iallfall tenke pisse" (Why not say 'piss,' when it is called 'piss', why not at least think 'piss').

It occurs to him that he is beginning to think with Tom's head, even using the folk form for "head," *hue* instead of his normal *hode*. Ironically he thinks: "Lektor Vegårdshei ligger og er folkelig til husbruk." (Lektor V. is being folksy for medicinal purposes). To which the author comments: "Frank Vegårdshei liker visst ikke seg selv i aften." (F. V. apparently doesn't like himself this evening).

Frank's encounter with Tom and their uneasy intimacy returns him to childhood. His acquired polish and education break down in this enforced self-assessment. It is the beginning of a schizophrenic breakdown which constitutes the novel. His mental collapse has its roots in the accident, his marriage, and the ulcer. But the insecurity of his personality is brought to a focus by his encounter with the uncomplicated, socially integrated man of the people, Tom Olsen, *stuert*.

The forms of address are skilfully manipulated to reveal the contrasting social roles of patient (regression to childhood), nurse (mother and lover), doctor (father and authority), companion (regression to lower social status). He reflects the educated man's vacillation between present and childhood status. The man's psychological insecurity is seen against the background of two sets of social rules, one basic and characteristic of the child and the folk, the other a superstructure acquired by the adult who enters into elite society. The rejection by more recent Norwegian youth of the formal pronouns must be seen as a rejection of the rules of elite society and the social dichotomy implied by them. A widespread academic trend toward stubbornly retaining one's folk dialect (or even acquiring one for the nonce) is also part of this rejection. Frank Vegårshei accepts Tom Olsen's rules.

Linguistically the choices involved may be described as a series of choices between unmarked and marked alternatives. The *t*-pronoun is unmarked, the *v*-pronoun marked [+ distance], a social meaning that is absent from the worlds of the child and the folk. To be sure, Tom Olsen vacillates between calling the nurse *du* and *dere*, the plural. This is an old second-person plural, going back to saga times and retained only among the folk (ON *pér* "ye"). The upper class long since adopted the Danish *De* "they" (after German *Sie*) as its formal pronoun. *Dere* is structurally equivalent to French *vous*, from which its function is derived (if not from Latin *vos*), but it reflects deference rather than distance.

Deference being an outmoded concept, the form is occasional and irregular in its use. Pronoun choice is of course obligatory, since sentences require subjects and objects. It can be avoided only by circumlocutions, as in traditional Swedish usage. But our text provides a special wheedling replacement of *t* by the plural *vi* "we", which we may call "sympathetic." It is used with children (and patients) in persuading them to do something they are reluctant to do. The plural pronoun can here be glossed "you and I," meaning that the speaker includes her/himself in the proposed action. Adults exchange the *t* with children, but have to choose *t* or *v* when they become adults. Here the nurse's role begins with an adult-child situation and progresses to normal adult-adult relation as the patient improves.

Pronominal usage eventually has to give way to name and/or title, if only to gain attention. The base form, historically and ontologically, is F. Its antiquity is reflected in the fact that kings have no other name. At the same time the king's position calls for the deference of complete suppression of the pronoun in favor of the third person address: *Deres majestet* ("Your majesty"). A similar usage for other titles is virtually obsolete and does not appear in our text. It could·have been used to the doctor, e.g. "Hva vil doktoren ha?" (What does the doctor wish?) Instead, titles are used for high status professions (*doktor, oberst, professor*), supplementing the pronouns. These may be preceded by the formal title *herr* or *fru* (Mr., Mrs.). A distinction is sometimes made between a wife who receives her husband's title (fru professor H.) and one who has a title of her own (professor fru H.).

The non-intimate situation requires a choice between L and $T L$ as vocatives. The nurse settles down to calling Frank by his last name alone, as does the doctor. Frank starts by calling Tom so, but is jovially corrected by Tom, who rejects the distance that is natural for Frank. The use of last name alone is a common Norwegian practice and may even be combined with the *t*-pronoun to mark an intermediate stage: familiarity rather than intimacy. Other alternatives of $T L$ are $F L$, as when Frank addresses his companion as "Tom Olsen", or T_2 and even $T_1 T_2$ in the case of the professions: "doktor" and "herr doktor," never the German triple-barreled "Herr Professor Doktor". In referring to our hero the author himself subtly varies between F, $F L$, and $T L$, the first as regular, the last to underline his role as educated person and professional teacher, with a hint of irony, the $F L$ to suggest his total personality.

We may now sum up the rules that govern the use of address forms. A flow chart will represent the available choices and the features of social behavior that govern them. We shall call the speakers X_1 as members of the folk (children, workers, farmers etc.), X_2 if they choose to associate themselves with the elite (officials, educated persons, urban bourgeoisie). Each choice is a node, and movement is from left to right. Features that determine choice are listed under each branch, omitting unmarked features. Essentially there are three choices: pronoun, title, and name, in that order. The pronouns are *v* for *vous* (*De*), *n p* for *nous* plural (*vi*), *t* for *tu* (*du*) and *t p* for *tu* plural (*dere*). The titles are T_1 for the formal Mr. (*herr*), Mrs. (*fru*), and Miss (*frøken*), abbr. hr., fru, frk. T_2 stands for professional names used in address like *doktor, oberst* etc. *F* is first name, *L* last name, and *N* nickname. The chart does not provide for sex differences or for the limitations on the use of formal titles. At the end of each line the possibilities of usage are indicated, with examples. Broken lines represent less usual alternatives.

Table 1

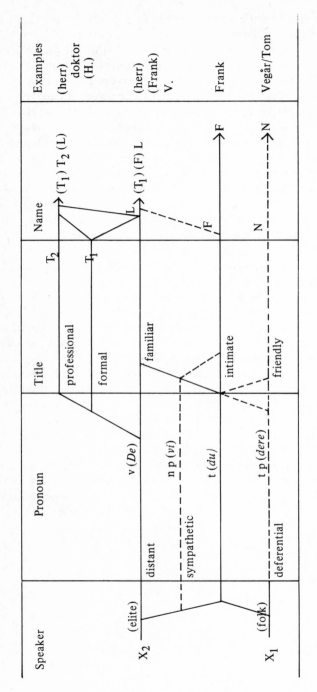

Chapter 18

Norwegian: Sexism

Costom drepr qvenna carla ofriki. (The tyranny of men destroys the chances of women)
Poetic Edda, ed. Bugge p. 304

Nora: Jeg tror at jeg er først og fremst et menneske, jeg, ligesåvel som du, – eller ialfald, at jeg skal forsøge på at bli'e det. (Nora: I believe that I am first and foremost a human being, I, just as well as you, – or at any rate, that I shall try to become one.)
Ibsen, *Samlede Værker* 1899, 6.333

A millenium or more separates the Guðrun of *Atlamál hin grønlenzku* from the Nora of Ibsen's *A Doll's House*, yet they are both concerned with women's lack of power in relation to men, the problem of women's liberation. Guðrun's words ring out with proverbial force. As the widow of Sigurd the Dragonslayer, she was not exactly a clinging vine. Her words were the mock-submissive prelude to her mass revenge on husband Atli for the slaying of her brothers. She proceeded to serve up their children to her husband as a festive meal, whereupon she murdered him in his bed.

Nora behaves in a more civilized way, but her words, too, are classic. By declaring that she has not been a *menneske*, she admits to a lower status than that of her husband. (It is at least amusing, if not significant, that the first translator, a Danish schoolteacher, rendered her words: "I think that I am first and foremost a man, like you.") But when Nora separates herself, it is a rejection that in modern terms is a kind of psychic murder.

Both women are capable of dissembling in order to manipulate their men, and in the showdown they are capable of coming out in the open and asserting their personalities. They typify what many have come to think of as the strong, Scandinavian woman, who is believed to have greater social freedom and economic power than other women of the west European world, on a par with and perhaps in advance of American women.

It may therefore come as a surprise to some that the Norwegian press of today, and certain parts of the academic world, are ringing with renewed calls for the assertion of women's rights. This *nyfeminisme* (neo-feminism), as it is often called, sounds like the echo of a battle that is being waged on many fronts in our own country as well. Norwegian women who have belonged to the older women's rights organizations are somewhat bewildered by the slogans of the new movement, uncertain whether it is indeed a continuation of the old women's movement or something entirely novel.

A woman's magazine which sounds like a Norwegian version of *Ms* has begun appearing under the ambitious name of *Sirene*. The word *sirene*, like its English and French counterparts, has the dual and hence ambiguous meanings of (1) "a beautiful, but false and dangerous woman" and (2) "a powerful sound-signaling apparatus whose tone resounds when steam or compressed air stream against a rotating disc with a series of holes." (*Norsk Riksmålsordbok*) This very punnish title, which embraces both the glamorous and the ominous aspects of womanhood, may serve as an example of how this new movement has begun to affect the Norwegian language.

My interest in the topic and my reason for bringing it to the attention of linguists is that both in Scandinavia and the United States militant women (and their male supporters) have put the finger on language as a factor in male dominance. To the extent that this is true, it becomes a question of sociolinguistics and involves sex as a factor in linguistic variation.

There is of course nothing new in the idea that men and women speak differently. A recent Norwegian study is by the linguist Magne Oftedal, "Notes on Language and Sex." (1973). He not only cites instances from various parts of the world, but also summarizes briefly the differences observed in his own local dialect of Norwegian from the south coastal town of Sandnes. Besides listing specific male/female differences on each linguistic level, he sums up the more general difference as one of greater "carefulness" on the part of women. He attributes this to their being liable to more severe judgments, especially on their "moral" behavior, but a number of his examples also point to women as spearheads of "refinement," a tendency to adopt urban expressions in preference to rural ones. He finds them "usually about one generation ahead of men in linguistic development."

Similar observations were made by another Norwegian dialectologist, Anders Steinsholt (1964), whose study and restudy of the rural dialect in an urbanizing neighborhood to Larvik is an outstanding sociolinguistic contribution. He writes: "I have spoken with several women in the transitional area (*brytingsområdet*) who use a more modern language [i.e. more urban] than their sons, and it is almost a rule that the members of a family divide into three groups linguistically: the father in one, the sons in one, and the mother and daughters in a third." (Steinsholt 1964: 31). He finds that men stop changing their language by age 30, while women are likely to go on adapting. He attributes this to the greater demands made on proper female behavior.

Amund B. Larsen, dean of modern Norwegian dialectologists, made a similar observation as long ago as 1912 in reference to nineteenth century dialect in Bergen: "Among the factors which now more than before contribute to preserving a careful (*omhyggelig*) language one must certainly mention the women of the cultivated classes." (Larsen and Stoltz 1912: 268). In 1935 Sommerfelt discussed the differences in male and female language, using examples from the plays of Ibsen. As the excellent sociolinguist he was, he rejected a biological explanation in favor of a social one: "Many things suggest that men and women were far more similar in physique in earlier ages, and the feminine charm and gentleness is not especially noticeable among many primitive peoples. It is conceivable that the difference will again be erased as the two sexes become more and more equal in modern society. Sports have already led many young girls of our day to use words and expressions that have previously been regarded as male and which their grandmothers would not have dreamt of using" (Sommerfelt 1936: 22).

Similar views are found in early studies from Denmark and France. Anker Jensen reported in 1898 on linguistic innovations in an urbanizing rural community near Århus in Denmark: the women were well in advance of men. In French Switzerland Gauchat found the same in his famous study of the "unité phonétique dans le patois d'une commune" at Charmey in 1905. Otto Jespersen summed up the evidence from that time in a classic study first published in 1906 entitled "Mands Sprog og Kvindes Tale" (Man's Language and Woman's Speech), later revised into a chapter in his book *Language* (1922: 237-254). His data were inadequate, and his views sound sexist to today's feminists; but he caught one significant generalization: that many of the differences were due to the division of labor between men and women in most societies. He wrote: "Many fundamental changes have occurred in our time with respect to the division of labor, and therefore also in education, so that one can predict that the relationship of the two sexes to linguistic activity will undergo extensive changes." (Jespersen 1906: 592).

Many of these old discoveries are being made anew, as often in linguistics. We find in a study of speech variation in the American Piedmont by Levine and Crockett (1966) that women are among those spearheading the "community's march toward the national norm." (1966: 97) Labov has also commented on women's "sensitivity to prestige forms": "the correct generalization then is not that women lead in linguistic change, but rather that the sexual differentiation of speech often plays a major role in the mechanism of linguistic evolution. ...We are dealing with some positive factor here, operating upon a subtle set of conventional social values." He speculates that this factor may be "an expressive posture which is socially more appropriate for one sex or the other." (Labov 1972: 304).

While the linguists so far cited have limited themselves to observing the social roles of the sexes, a young Norwegian social psychologist, Rolf M. Blakar, at the University of Oslo, has taken up the cudgels in behalf of women. He sees their linguistic roles as one expression of the ways in which language determines and conserves the inequities of society. He has embodied his views in a small textbook, *Språk er makt* "Language is power", (1973) and several articles, which have caused a bit of a stir.

Blakar finds that the Norwegian language is essentially sexist in the sense that it sees the entire world in male terms and assigns to women an inferior, dependent position. Not content to accept this as the way things are, he envisages a revolution in the social conventions that regulate the relations of the sexes. In fairness to Blakar I note that he is not so naive as to think that social realities can be changed merely by relabeling them (p. 63). Sexism is only one of several causes he uncovers through an analysis of the power relations expressed in language. He is aware of similar biases in the treatment of differences in class, age, and region. And he is peculiarly sensitive to the discrimination he finds in the treatment of Norway's national minority language, the Nynorsk-Norwegian in which he writes.

The examples Blakar presents to bolster his claims are amusing enough to make his arguments at least readable, though their clear agitatorial purpose may turn some readers off. He offers evidence from (a) the use of titles of address, (b) the descriptors of occupation, (c) the synonyms for "man" and "woman," (d) word association tests, and (e) the listing of husbands and wives in official registers.

A professor's wife is liable to be introduced as *fru professor Hansen*, but what if she is a professor in her own right? And in that case, why should not her husband be called *herr professor Hansen* even if he has no right to such a title? What we in English call a "working woman" is known in Norwegian as an *yrkeskvinne*; why is there not a word *yrkesmann?* In English we have "career women"; why not also "career men." Synonyms, he finds, are not only more numerous for women, but also quite a bit less complimentary than for men. An intellectual woman, for example, is a "bluestocking"; an intellectual man is apparently just intellectual.

In a sampling of one thousand Norwegian men and women, responses to the stimulus word "man" included such words as "work," "worker," and "career," while "woman" elicited such words as "sex," "bed," and "mother." In the 1972 official register of marriages every husband-to-be is listed by name and title, while every wife-to-be is listed by name only. Blakar contends that these and other practices of a similar nature determine the views of the new generations as they learn the language and are gradually socialized. These biases help to channel the activities of children and determine the goals they set for themselves in growing up to adulthood.

On the basis of this analysis Blakar proceeds to offer countermeasures to neutralize the discrimination revealed by these ways of speaking. His first proposal is what has come to be called "consciousness raising" in this country: to make users of the language aware of the ways in which their habits of speaking reveal traditional and mostly unconscious discrimination. This is true not only of such obvious occupational discriminations as *stortingsmann* ("congressman") vs. *vaskekone* ("washer woaman"). It applies also to such apparently neutral occupational terms as *doctor, judge*, or *pastor* for which "he" is the standard pronoun, while terms like *nurse, gossip*, or *virgin* are associated with "she".

He proposes a technique of reversal by which one will speak of a "male judge" or even "a male chairman" to emphasize the implicit discrimination in the usual term. In a series of prose poems he exemplifies his technique (pp. 80-83); I include one example:

FRIDAGEN	DAY OFF
Han hadde fri i går	He had the day off yesterday
– yrkesmannen.	– the career man.
Derfor gjekk han som sladremann	So he went around as a gossip man
frå hus til hus	from house to house
og hygga seg saman med alle dei andre	and had a cozy time with all the
skravlemennnene og kaffemennene	other chatterbox men and the
	coffee drinkers
i bygda.	in the community.

While my translation is obviously inadequate because of the lack of certain expressions in English, the idea will be clear, and anyone can supply examples from English.

The concept underlying Blakar's argument, that "language is power," is of course not new. It was formulated by Lewis Carroll in *Through the Looking Glass*, when Alice protested at Humpty-Dumpty's contention that he could make a word mean just what he chose it to mean. "The question is," said Alice, "whether you *can* make words mean so many different things." "The question is," said Humpty-Dumpty, "which is to be master – that's all."

In his book *Black Power* (1967), Stokely Carmichael quoted this passage and went on to apply it to black liberation: "We shall have to struggle for the right to create our own terms through which to define ourselves and our relationship to the society and to have these terms recognized." "Those who have the right to define are masters of the situation." (Carmichael and Hamilton 1967: 37). The replacement of "Negro" by "Black" is a paradigmatic example of such a redefinition. But the slogan "Black is beautiful" would hardly have won such resonance if it had not been for the Supreme Court decision on desegregation in 1954 and the freedom marches led by Martin Luther King. Even the relabeling involved has not solved the race problem; many have not accepted it, as Rafky (1970) found in studying "the semantics of negritude" at an integrated American university. The use of such terms as "black" or "Afro-American" expressed attitudes that were regarded as either "liberal," "alienated," or "militant."

Stimulated by the advances of Black Power, the feminist movement in our country has adopted the attack on sexist language as one of its strategies. In some cases they have gone deeper than the lexicon and attacked such basic parts of the language as the pronominal system, which in Indo-European languages forces us to mark sex in the third person. It is no doubt too facile to reply that women can hardly be said to have a higher position in societies where languages like Japanese, Chinese, Eskimo, or Tamil are spoken. Linguists have offered a weightier objection, which turns on the concept of "markedness," as proposed by Jakobson and others of the Prague School. In the opposition man/woman the noun "man" and the pronoun "he" are the unmarked members of the opposition and can therefore be used generically whenever the contrast is neutralized.

I am not sure whether it is any comfort to women to know that they are the "marked" member of this pair, since it quite simply means that they are set off from men by virtue of a single feature, which we can only describe as [+sexuality]. Because this feature is ultimately biological in its base, it cannot be eliminated. But its effects need not have spread throughout our social life in the pervasive way it does. One may say with the French, "Vive la différence," but only so long as the difference does not obscure the common humanity of men and women.

My own comment on the arguments advanced by Blakar and others is that even though some of them are one-sided, unreasonable, and unrealistic, they deal with a real and an important problem. We have such well-written articles as Robin Lakoff's "Language and Woman's Place" (1973), which goes no farther than to urge teachers of language to be aware of the discriminations implicit in language. Her article is also notable in representing one of the few realizations by current linguists that sentences may be "acceptable" or "unacceptable" for reasons entirely outside the grammar. (Lakoff 1973: 77).

Interesting also is a thoughtful survey of recent research presented by Virginia Clark, as well as an excellent annotated bibliography by Thorne and Henley (1975). Much of it reminds me of the General Semanticists of the 1930's and 1940's, headed by Korzybski, Hayakawa, and Stuart Chase. Their concern with "the tyranny of words" was not balanced by an understanding of "the freedom of words." There is much that reminds one of the doctrines of linguistic relativity, of which more below. Blakar's view that "language reflects and conserves social realities" is in line with this idea, which overlooks our vast potential for linguistic innovation and creativeness.

My feeling is that Blakar's claim about language as a conserver of social realities is either a truism or a trick. Most of the discrimination of which women complain today involves that they are typed in certain occupations and virtually excluded from others. But when women are assigned roles as home-makers and men the role of career-makers, it is not because language puts it that way. The language expresses, if somewhat conservatively, the realities as the vast number of men and women have seen it down to our day. As long as this is true, it is good that language should tell us so. When it changes, as it may and should, the language will respond, as it already has. Language as the preserver of tradition is not bad until we begin to discover that the tradition it preserves is bad.

That this one has bad aspects can hardly be denied, and I should be the last to do so. In a perceptive note to Lakoff's article, Hymes writes that the stereotypes of sex roles may have been as much of a detriment to men as to women: "The association of male creativity in the arts with effeminacy is a well-known instance" (Lakoff 1973: 79). To this one can add that teaching is not entirely free from the same problem. Anyone who has come up through the American public school system can testify that to grow up with bookish interests is to qualify for epithets like "sissy" and "teacher's pet." So it is true that language can reflect prejudice and contempt; but it can equally express admiration and support, not so speak of affection and human warmth.

When Blakar and others therefore speak of language as an instrument of power, it seems to me that they are thinking too exclusively of political and economic achievement. This no doubt says something about our western standards of success. But the "power" that goes with being "male" in the linguistic stereotypes brings anxieties and responsibilities that many men would be glad to escape. The "powerlessness" that goes with being "female" in the same stereotypes has been turned to account by women since the dawn of time. Perhaps there are some advantages is being the "marked member" after all; I suspect that the distinction is complementary rather than contrastive.

I began with a quotation from the *Edda* and *A Doll's House*. I wish to close with one from that well-known Swedish lover and hater of women, August Strindberg. In *Miss Julie* (1888) the strong-willed heroine tells about her mother: "She was brought up in the doctrines of her time about equality, the liberation of women and all that sort of thing, and she had a definite aversion to marriage. ...And on the estate men were ordered to do women's work, and the women to do men's work, – with the result that the property was about to go under, and we became the laughing stock of the community."

Miss Julie's mother was ahead of her time; but will her time ever come?

Chapter 19

Norwegian: A Frontier

When the first Norwegians arrived in South Dakota, the area was still a battleground between the Sioux Indians and the United States Government. A treaty of 1859 had opened the land to white settlers, and in 1861 Dakota Territory was created by Congress. The bloody Sioux War of 1862 in Minnesota led to the removal of the Minnesota Sioux to the Missouri River in 1863. Beginning in 1855, the government had established a series of forts on the Missouri. These performed the dual function of protecting white settlers and of feeding the displaced Indians.

The accompanying map shows where the major forts were located in relation to the cities which eventually grew up in the area (Haugen 1931). Through 1872 Sioux City, Iowa was the terminus of the railroad. It was little more than a collection of stores and homes on the river bottoms near the confluence of the Sioux River with the Missouri.

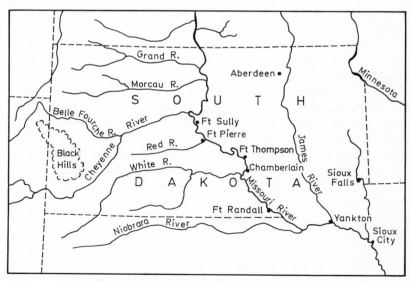

Missouri River Forts in the Seventies

Its growth coincided with the coming to America of large numbers of Norwegian immigrants, who found that land was already taken in the older settlements in Illinois, Wisconsin, Iowa, and Minnesota. (Qualey 1938: 130-148) So they wended their way out to the open prairies of the new Dakota Territory. Many of them found employment in Sioux City and formed the nucleus of a long-enduring urban community in that city. I should perhaps explain that this town was the place of my birth and for many years the home of my parents.

Many Norwegians spread into the nearby area in what became South Dakota, made their land claims and developed solidly Norwegian rural communities in the eastern strip, especially in the southeastern corner of the state. By 1900 they amounted to 12.8 per cent of the total population of South Dakota. But before they could build proper homes and become the prosperous farmers of a later age, most of them needed to earn the cash they could get by manual labor for American employers. In the 1870's the chief employer in this wilderness was the United States Government, which needed blacksmiths, lumberjacks, and carpenters, as well as just plain common labor to sustain the forts.

This was the area in which it became my good fortune to do my first field work on the Norwegian language in America. This work was entirely incidental to the historical research of my mother, Kristine Haugen (1879-1956). She was then editor of an annual publication known as *Opdalslagets aarbok*. This annual, which she edited from 1928 to 1935, was the organ of *Opdalslaget*, one of the many organizations with ties to the homeland that were formed among American Norwegians, collectively known as *bygdelag* (Lovoll 1975). The members consisted of immigrants (and some of their children) from the community of Oppdal (as it is written today) in the county of South Tröndelag.

Group emigration from this secluded inland mountain valley began in the 1860's, as part of the post-Civil War migration wave. The first known group to arrive came to Sioux City on May 16, 1869, and duly combined a celebration of their safe arrival with a commemoration of Norway's Constitution Day on May 17. Many of them spread out into Dakota Territory and in a few years one could speak of an Oppdal community in the farming area between Yankton and Sioux Falls, particularly by the small towns of Volin and Irene that sprang up later. The community stretched northwards to Viborg, where it met a settlement of Danes from Jutland (Haugen 1976b: 42-49).

The contents of the annual published by Opdalslaget were, in my mother's time, primarily of a historical-biographical nature. By letter and by personal interviews she gathered data on people from Oppdal, chiefly the living early settlers. The results were written up and printed in standard Norwegian

(*Bokmål*) in the form of biographies or obituaries of the grand old men and women of the community.

My share in this, aside from acting as chauffeur on these totally unsubsidized safaris, was to record as best I could the words that fell from the lips of these ancient narrators. The experience was enthralling to a young man who had already discovered the study of Scandinavian dialects and languages as the main ambition of his life.

The language I heard was a wholly unselfconscious example of a local Norwegian dialect (which was also my own), laced with bits and pieces of book Norwegian plus the remarkably distorted English words picked up by these people in their contacts with Americans. In many cases the form showed that they were learned at a time when the Norwegian pioneers had not yet mastered any form of English. Fort Sully (as I later learned that it was spelled) was regularly pronounced /fort šale/ as if it were "Fort Charley." The government, their employer, was /guvvament-en/, reflecting the common American "guvament", with the Norwegian masculine definite article hooked on the end.

While there may have been recording devices available in 1929, the summer when I did most of my scribal work, I had no access to them and jotted down from dictation the narratives which my mother would use. She needed only to get the content and would then rewrite it into proper Norwegian for publication. But I had already had a year of graduate work and had done a good deal of reading in phonetics, so I did my best to render the words as I heard them.

The result was hardly adequate for a true phonetic transcription, but my jottings reflect in a broad way the variations from dialect to standard Norwegian to the English of our speakers. The interviews were conducted in Norwegian by my mother, for this was still the dominant language in the community. I had already visited the area, spending summers there with cousins, who formed our base of operations. There were also the annaul summer meetings of the society itself, usually held in the assembly hall of Augustana Academy in Canton, later to be merged with Augustana College in Sioux Falls, South Dakota. The young people of my own age were mostly quite bilingual, speaking Norwegian (dialect) at home and English at school and to outsiders. We were not outsiders.

The results of our joint expedition were eventually published in *Opdalslagets Aarbok* 1933. As Haugen 1931 they are only in part available in English for the benefit of the descendants of those whose lives are here portrayed. While the contents are often humdrum, the early settlers had much to tell about the inhumanly harsh conditions, particularly before there were roads or adequate means of either transportation or living. It was rough country, dominated by cowboys and soldiers, often in conflict with Indians and entrepreneurs of the saloonkeeper type, who made their living by providing for the social needs of men on the edge of the wilderness.

The preceding is by way of prelude to some notes and comments on the American-Norwegian contact dialect that I recorded in that summer of 1929. While I still have my original notes, they could hardly be published as authentic linguistic texts in view of their imperfections. I have since published a volume in Norway on the Oppdal dialect, to which I refer the interested reader (Haugen 1982).

The Norwegian-American material that will here be presented is from the narration of Halvor O. Aune (1846-1932), who emigrated to America in 1869, followed by his brother Ole Lie in 1870. (Obituaries in *Opdalslagets Aarbok* 1936-38: 59). I have it in two versions, evidently told on two different occasions. I shall present them exactly as recorded and discuss the differences. They throw light on problems of language contact, while providing a key to the sociocultural landscape in which these Norwegian farm youths had to orient themselves.

The two brothers had difficulty in finding work in Sioux City, so together with a number of other Norwegians they made their way into the wilderness of Dakota and found employment at one or another of the government forts. Aune dictated a very long narrative (it took some ten hours to get it all down), full of lively anecdotes, amusing but occasionally less than plausible. The following text is one short sample. As Text 1 it is part of the long, dicated narrative. As Text 2 it is told freely, in a form much closer to his natural speech. Loanwords are italicized, loanshifts are starred.

Text 1

[Halvor and his brother Ole returned from Fort Sully to Yankton in the spring of 1871, out of work.] Så fikk vi brev fra *basen* at vi skulle komo opp igjen, men kun e og Ola, oss villa'n ha. Så skulle vi spare penger, vi skulle gå tri hundrede mil* te foss. Og så ble vi sårføtte. Så kom vi te et *rensj* en aften, en fransmann som ha ei *skvå*. Hann ha *salon*, o de kosta fem o tjug *sent* glase, du mått betal før du fekk fengra i glase, de va itt no kreditt å fo der. Så mått vi stoppe over natten* der. Så si franskmann, vask deres fødder godt, her er såpe, skur dem godt. Da vi var færdi med de, kom hann me en stor vaskebolle*, hann to vist en par *gallona*, full me *viski*. No ska du vask føtn me de derre. Så sa e te Ole, de bli en kostbar vask. De ikke non ann rå, de får berre skure, vi må *rønne resken*. Vi vaska oss, vi låg der og kvilte godt og bena blev *all rait*. Så sier je te Ola, gad vite om hann slo vekk den *viskien*. Vi så efter, og hann slo den ikke vekk. Hann fyllte den vist i flasken igjen, og nogen fekk dyrt betale vasken vor. Vi betalte om morgenen for *brækfest* og seng og *søppel*, en daler* og en halv på kvar. Så spurte jeg hva *viskien* skull kost. Inginteng, sa'n. (See version in Haugen 1939; 119; 1975: 111)

(Then we got a letter from the *boss* that we should come back up, but only Ole and I, he wanted to have us. So we were going to save money, we would walk three hundred miles* on foot. And then we got sore feet. So we came to a *ranch* one evening, a Frenchman who had a *squaw*. He had a *saloon*, and it cost twenty-five *cents* a glass, you had to pay before you got your fingers on the glass, there was no credit to be had there. So we had to stop over night* there. Then the Frenchman says, "Wash your feet well, here's soap, scour them well." When we were through with that, he brought a big wash bowl*, it took at least a couple of *gallons*, full of *whisky*. "Now you wash your feet in this here." Then I said to Ole, "This is going to be an expensive washing. But there's no other way, it'll have to do, we have to *run the risk*. We washed, we slept there and rested well, and our feet were *all right*. Then I said to Ole, "I wonder if he poured that *whisky* out." We watched, and he did not pour it out. He probably filled it back in the bottle, and someone had to pay through the nose for our washing. In the morning we paid for *breakfast* and bed and *supper*, a dollar* and a half each. Then I asked what the *whisky* would cost. "Nothing," he said.)

Text 2

Hann Ola bror min o e, oss gjekk fir honnder mil.* Så va de en dag oss vart så sårføtt, oss ha vel *kjippe* sko, au. Så kom oss åt en *rench*. Den *ranch*manden* ha ord for ikke å være mors beste barn. Hann ha no ei *skva*, kanske fler. Så sa'n oss skull ta tå oss sko'n, og så fann 'n ti et tå sæ sto'r kvi't vaskarfatom som dem enno bruke og fyllt med *viski*. Så sa'n oss skull vask føtn ti di. Minn da vesst oss itt ka oss skull gjårrå. Dæ kjem te å kost oss nå, ditte her, Ola, sa e. For ett lite glas kosta fem og tjug *sent*, og de gjekk mange slike glas ti di fate. Da oss ha vaska oss, tømt han det på ei krokk, og sia sælt hann det vist. Om morgon skull oss beta'l for oss. De var femti *sent* for losji og femti *sent* for mat. Men kva skull *viskien* kost, spurt oss. Inginn teng, svara'n. Menn da tøkt e de tok oss rekti godt. ... Og bena vart go. Sia ha e godt for den mann, sjøl om hann ha ord for itt å vårå tå di bæ'st.

(My brother Ola and I, we walked four hundred miles.* Then it happened one day that our feet got very sore, I suppose we had *cheap* shoes, too. Then we came to a *ranch*. The *rancher* there had the reputation of not being of the best kind. He had a *squaw*, perhaps several. Then he told us to take off our shoes, and he brought out one of those big white *washbowls* that they still use and filled it with *whisky*. Then he told us to wash our feet in it. But then we didn't know what we should do. "This is going to cost us something, this here, Ola," I said. For one little glass cost twenty-five *cents*, and it took many glasses to fill that bowl. When we had washed, he poured it back into a jug, and later on I guess he sold it. In the morning we went to pay up. It was fifty *cents* for lodging and fifty *cents* for food. But what did the *whisky* cost, we asked. "Nothing," he replied. But then I felt real good about it [...]

And our feet were healed. After that I had a good feeling about this man, even though he had the reputation of not being of the best sort.)

Neither transcription shows such phonetic details as the palatalization of *ll, nn, tt,* or the retroflex flapped *l* (used once in *supper,* written *ł*). With editing, Text 1 could pass as nineteenth century Dano-Norwegian, with some bookish forms, e.g. *deres fødder* "your feet" (for *føttene*), *kun* "only" (for *bare*), *morgenen* "the morning" (for *mornen*), *nogen* "someone" (for *noen*) etc. But the dialect substratum also shows through, e.g. *komo* "come" (for *komme*), *tri* "three" (for *tre*), *te foss* "on foot" (for *til fots*), *ha* "had" (for *hadde, kosta* "cost" (for *kostet*), apocope in *mått betal* "had to pay" for *måtte betale*) and *skull kost* "should cost" (for *skulle koste*). There are alternations between dialect and standard, e.g. *fekk/fikk* "got", *skull/skulle* "should", *Ole/Ola, itt/ikke* "not", *e/jeg* "I" etc. Our speaker has 13 instances of apocopated *-e* but drops it in 6. Weak preterites keep dialect *-a* (*villa, vaska*), but only some nouns do (*fengra* "the fingers", *bena* "the feet" vs. *natten* "the night", *flasken* "the bottle".) Consistently non-dialectal are the use of *vi* "we" (for *oss*) and suppression of the dative.

Aside from the loanwords the text is unmistakably Norwegian, intended to be literary standard. As he dictated, he was in effect reading from memory, in a form appropriate to a written account (which he is known to have composed). But his modest schooling and his life as a manual laborer made his diglossia imperfect.

Text 2 gives an entirely different picture. Here the *oss* for *vi* and the dative are not suppressed. Apocope is regular and the circumflex is here marked with an apostrophe (*sto'r kvi't* "(the) big white" for *store kvite*). The minor deviations from the dialect are in the direction of literary style: *men* "but" (for *minn*), *var* "was" for *va, ta* "take" for *tå, spurt* "asked" (for *spor*), *mors beste barn* "mother's best child" (a literary quotation).

The English loans are of virtually the same order in both texts. They show some minor variation in form (*rench/rensh/ranch-, skvå/skva* (possibly due to transcription). Note also *en* vs. *et ranch,* usually the former. Norwegians had trouble distinguishing *ranch* from *wrench.* Other phonetic adaptations are evident in *rønne* "run" and *søppeł* "supper", *resken* "the risk". *Salon* "saloon" and *gallona* "gallons" have stress on the first syllable and a long *o,* i.e. spelling pronunciations. Consonants are geminated after short vowels in *gallona, rønne, søppeł* and *kjippe.* Grammatical adaptation is complete in *rønne resken* "(to) run the risk", *kjippe* "cheap" plural, *gallona* "gallons". *Squaw* is correctly feminine.

Only the more obvious loanshifts are noted: the Norwegian *daler* was inevitable for American "dollar", *mil* the American *mile.* Loanshifts are *over natten* "over night" (for *natten over*); *vaskebolle* "wash bowl" (in Text 2 he uses the correct *vaskarfat; ranchmanden* "the ranch man", i.e. rancher.

Most of the loans are key terms in the new landscape: land measured in *miles*, liquids in *gallons*, payment in *dollars* and *cents*, meals known as *break-fast* and *supper*, *ranches* with Frenchmen who had *squaws* and ran *saloons*. It was a perilous country where you *ran risks* and hoped it would be *all right*. Poor immigrants could get only *cheap* shoes. Words like *boss* and *whiskey* were known back home, but were clearly reinforced in America.

The narrative quality also differs: Text 1 is more circumstantial and probably more accurate, but Text 2 is superior as a narrative. It establishes the saloon keeper as a diamond in the rough, and the footbath becomes a vignette in character study.

These small samples show that Norwegians did their part in the winning of the West. They also offer illuminating evidence of how radically the speech situation can alter a speaker's language, inducing a virtual inhibition when the narrator believes he must elevate his language. They show how the language is reshaped to meet new situations and how speakers follow norms for bilingual behavior.

Chapter 20

Ethnicity: Swedes and Norwegians

To most Americans it is impossible to distinguish the emigrants from the two countries that occupy the Scandinavian peninsula. I am often asked: "Are Norwegians on the east or the west?" Among some there is a lingering memory of squabbles long since past, but this has become a topic for stale jokes. But it is actually a topic of some interest, and we shall here present a survey.

The closeness of the two groups is reflected in the existence of popular songs that appear in double versions, one Norwegian and one Swedish. One of the most widely known (and sung) is a sentimental ballad that begins with the following verse:

Farwäl du moder Swea, nu reser jag från dig
Och tackar dig af hjertat, för det du fostrat mig.
Mig bröd du gaf så ringa, det ofta ej förslog,
Fast mången af den waran, du gifwit mer än nog. (Jonsson 1974)

According to the ballad scholar Bengt R. Jonsson, it appeared in broadside form at least nineteen times between 1892 and 1900. But it also appeared in a Norwegian version, which was no less popular, with appropriate modifications:

Farvel du Moder Norge, nu reiser jeg fra dig,
og siger dig saa mange Tak fordi du fostret mig.
Du blev for knap i Kosten imod din Arbeidsflok,
men dine lærde Sønner du giver mer end nok. (Amundsen and Kvideland 1975)

(Farewell, oh mother Sweden/Norway, I leave you now/and give you hearty thanks because you fostered me./You gave me little bread, it did often not suffice,/but others you gave plenty, more than you gave me. The Norwegian version deviates in the last two lines: You were stingy in providing for your working men/but to your learned sons you give more than enough.)

According to the Norwegian ballad scholars Amundsen and Kvideland it is impossible to say whether the ballad is originally Norwegian or Swedish, or who has composed it. But no one can doubt that it is the same ballad. It illustrates plainly both the similarity that existed between Swedish and Norwegian emigration and the difference that made it necessary to translate it from one language to the other.

More examples could be found, the most striking example being the ballad well-known both in Norwegian and Swedish, with the refrain "Skade at Amerika ligge skal så langt herfra." (A shame that America should lie so far away). But this song turns out to have a well-known author, the Danish Hans Christian Andersen!

The great migration from Scandinavia to America has been a topic of some interest in recent years and has occasioned great jubilees, e.g. the celebration of America's bicentennial as well as the hundred and fifty years since the beginning of Norwegian emigration. It has also been stimulated by Vilhelm Moberg's epic treatment of Swedish emigration from Småland to Minnesota in a four-volume novel, and by the two brilliant films by Jan Troell built upon the novel. (Moberg 1949-1959).

A Swedish Emigration Institute has been created in Växsjö and there are similar institutions in Norway and Denmark. Nordic historians have shown an intense, if belated interest in the emigrants. Professor Folke Hedblom of Uppsala University has undertaken a series of recording expeditions to save the last remnants of American Swedish.

But we must not overlook that the emigrants themselves began writing their own history a century ago, and that American scholars of Nordic ancestry have done yeoman work. My main point here, however, is that it has nearly always been Norwegian-Americans who have done research in Norwegian immigration and Swedish-Americans who have studied Swedish immigration. Only in the rarest cases has anyone tried to see it from a general Scandinavian point of view. We lack a Nordic perspective. No one has written the history of Scandinavianism in America.

The first problem is that of "nationalism," which in America has made its appearance under the name of "ethnicity." It is my hypothesis that the nationalism which Norwegians and Swedes bore with them on arrival had to be weakened to ethnicity under the pressure of American opinion before they could begin to feel like Scandinavians.

The inability of Americans to distinguish them has been a factor of irritation: they are known as "Swedes," even as "dumb Swedes." In a Norwegian-American story a girl is insulted when an Irishman calls her "a nice Swedish flicka." "Nothing irritated her more than being called Swedish." (Skaardal 1974: 102) The special traits of each nationality are held to be childish and even comical. It is part of American folklore that Norwegians and Swedes are implacable enemies, a topic for witticisms of the type, "What's a Swede/ a Norwegian?" "A Norwegian/a Swede with his brains knocked out." Or the visitor from Sweden who is shown Indians and observes that they have them in Sweden, too, only there they're called Norskies. Or a popular verse about "ten thousand Swedes ran through the weeds, chased by one Norwegian."

Such "witticisms" were no doubt an echo of the actual unpleasantness that arose during the years when the Swedo-Norwegian union broke up, from

1890 to 1905. But they did not come from Scandinavia and were not created by Scandinavians. They are an American product that stems from a general contempt for the various European nationalities. If anything they have tended to bring Scandinavians closer together.

One cannot deny that Scandinavians resemble each other biologically, that they have closely related languages, that they have a common religious development from belief in the Norse gods to Catholicism to Lutheranism, and that they have grown out of an authoritarian into a democratic way of life, from bureaucratic rule to social democracy, from poverty and ignorance to affluence and education.

What is it then that actually separates them? First and foremost a nationalism that builds in part on the political development from the time of Danish Christian II and Swedish Gustavus Vasa. From loyalty to the king has grown a national feeling, pride in one's own tradition, ill will or ignorance about the others'. Nationalism in the modern sense is really something new, that hardly goes very far behind the French Revolution. It is far from a natural given, as the Romantics believed. It came with popular education, brainwashing if you will, to which we are all exposed in school and in all the organs that the state controls.

It has been maintained that the emigrants to a great extent lacked national feeling when they left. They abandoned family and friends, a local society that they well might love and miss abroad, but they only became nationalists when they got to America (Lindmark 1971: 37). It was the contact with other nationalities that made them ethnically self-conscious. The very pattern of settlement was local, determined by the occupational opportunities they found, often guided by a desire to live near relatives and friends. (Cf. "the stock effect" discussed by Carlsson in Runblom and Norman 1976: 138). Therefore it turned out not only that Norwegians and Swedes lived apart, but also local fellow citizens from the rural (or urban) districts.

The so-called "settlements" were often built up by families or clans, much like the society we see mirrored in the Icelandic sagas. Family cohesion is at one end of the continuum that has nationalism at the other. Between them lies that whole area of modern thinking about loyalty and group solidarity that has been called "ethnicity."

The word builds on the Greek word for "people," *ethnos,* but as a technical term it was launched in 1950, as a synonym of "national origin." (McGuire 1950; Hollingshead 1950). In recent years it has won popularity as a term that replaces "race" or "nationality," which are no longer applicable. (Glazer and Moynihan 1975). It may express itself in loyalty to one's kin, extending no farther than genealogical research. Or it may search out contacts with the spiritual heritage of one's old homeland and reawaken interest in the language and literature that was lost. This is what has been called "the revival of ethnicity," a feature of modern American life. The interest has even extended to the homeland itself (Lindmark 1971).

I may illustrate the problems involved by reference to my childhood home in Sioux City, Iowa. My parents and I were not enthusiastic about trends that in 1918 would deny us the right to maintain our ancestral heritage. We belonged to a church that still had a Norwegian service each Sunday and a Norwegian-born pastor who not only had confirmed me but also lent us books from his well-stocked library. My mother, a teacher from Norway and a warm-hearted patriot, entered me in a Norwegian young people's society where recent immigrants from Norway were welcomed.

Our church belonged to the United Norwegian Lutheran Church. A block away lay the rival church that belonged to Hauge's Synod. And down the street lay the imposing Swedish Augustana Synod church, not very far from the more modest Swedish Mission Church which became the Swedish Covenant Church. In this little area, within sight, lay four different Lutheran choices, all built by Scandinavian Lutherans, but sharply separated by national and doctrinal differences. I can count on the fingers of one hand the number of times we went to the Swedish churches.

Other contacts, however, brought us together with Swedes, especially cross marriages. I read my first Swedish books in the local library. But the churches stood there as a defiant reminder of the cleavages in Scandinavian nationality and doctrine. I can say with assurance that no Norwegian or Swedish is now preached and that the synods involved either are or will soon be united in an American Lutheran Church.

If we turn from my microcosm to the macrocosm that is constituted by the whole Scandinavian immigrant society in America, we see the same splinterings. In her book *The Divided Heart* (1974) Dorothy Skaardal has boldly treated Scandinavian-American literature together. But she is aware of the special homeland loyalty: "Immigrants of the three nationalities felt special kinship and sympathy with each other, but not a sense of cultural union. They shared parallel fates, but each group stood or fell alone." (Skaardal 1974: 88)

That their fates have been parallel is clear if one considers Helge Nelson's map of Swedish settlement in America (1943, vol. 2). If one compares it with Qualey's of Norwegian settlement, one notes at once the remarkable concentration on the prairies of the Midwest, with Minnesota as its center. (Qualey 1938). The Norwegian historian Svalestuen has prepared a Nordic Emigration Atlas (1971), which suggests a similar set of causes of emigration. It was a movement of small farmers and impoverished craftsmen who were needed to cultivate the newly acquired expanses of the Middle West. Other factors, such as religious distempers, played in, but mainly it was America's cheap soil and good wages.

Norwegian emigration is earlier than Swedish because Norway faced the Atlantic and had less soil than Sweden. Not until 1880 did the Swedes surpass the Norwegians in number. Emigration culminated in both countries in 1882, and by 1910 there were about fifty per cent more first-generation Swedes than Norwegians in the United States. One result is that while Norwegians "dominate" in Wisconsin, they are less numerous in Minnesota. The map also shows that Swedes have spread more widely. While Norwegians led in states like North and South Dakota, Montana, and Oregon, and approached the Swedes in Washington, the Swedes had leadership in a more southerly belt covering Illinois, Nebraska and Kansas. They are also well represented in New England, and in cities where there are few Norwegians, like Boston, Rockford, St. Paul, Jamestown, Worcester, and Detroit. In 1900 there were twice as many Swedish industrial workers and only one half as many in agriculture as the Norwegians. In 1910 65 per cent of all Norwegians lived in the Middle West, but only 45 per cent of the Swedes (Runblom and Norman 1976: 246-7).

The history of Scandinavian institutions shows many examples of cooperation, including marriage patterns: Swedes and Norwegians married each other oftener than any other nationalities.

But it is clear that the languages, in spite of their modest differences, were an essential barrier. The key was such words as *norskdom* and *svenskhet,* which could no more be mixed than oil and water.

Both languages struggled against the overwhelming influence of English, which not only drove them out of entrenched positions, but actually colored them while they were still in use. A Swedish poet described what he called "the new mother tongue":

I *ståret* tar hon allting på 'krita',	In the *store* she takes all on credit,
Hon är för god att en menska *chita.*	Too good to *cheat* any person.
Hon går til *mitingen,* vår Fredrika,	She goes to the *meeting,* our Fredrika,
Der 'vangelistar' så fromma skrika.	Where 'vangelists piously shriek.
Hon lefver lyckligt. Man henne prisar	She lives happily, they praise her
För hennes ögon, − två fina *pisar;*	For her eyes, − two fine *pieces;*
Men jag mest prisar den nya svenska,	But I will praise the new Swedish,
som är så olik den fosterländska.	Which is so unlike the old country's.

(Skarstedt 1890).

The transition to English, which follows precisely the same course in both groups, becomes to some extent a unifying factor. This first became possible in politics, which was English from the start. Studies of elections in Minnesota and Wisconsin show that Norwegians and Swedes voted together (Carlsson 1970; Norman 1974). A Swedish observer in 1910 claimed that the Norwegians were more active in politics than the Swedes (Koch 1910: 363). But it is clear that the Norwegian Knute Nelson would never have become senator without Swedish votes, nor would the Swedish John Lind have become governor of Minnesota without the Norwegians. In battling the Irish and the Anglo-Saxons they found a common cause.

The specifically national qualities of Norwegians and Swedes prevented them from forming a united front until their linguistic differences had ceased to matter. The social features are the ones that disappear first: language, manners, tradition, politics, literature. What they could take with them into American life was their physique, their diligence, their reliability, their religion, and to some extent their onomastic tradition. The ethnicity that remains is strongly diluted, even if it may include a sense of family, but it is more likely to be Nordic than national.

Chapter 21

Relativity

A perennial topic of discussion among American students of language has been the theory described by Benjamin Whorf as "linguistic relativity," also known as the 'Sapir-Whorf hypothesis." It might rather be called "linguistic determinism," since it maintains in effect that people's thinking is determined by their language.

The theory has been subjected to severe criticism and is at present less popular than one that stresses *universalism*. This view emphasizes the features common to all languages and is less interested in the peculiarities of individual languages.

There is much to be said for each of these complementary views, but a one-sidedness that claims truth for only one of them is misleading and intellectually dangerous. In this essay I am interested in analyzing some of Whorf's insights and suggesting why they went wrong. They may be out of favor now, but they are certain to reappear in one guise or another.

Whorf was an insurance adjustor who came under the influence of linguist Edward Sapir. He made a name for himself by relating the grammatical and lexical structures of certain American Indian languages (chiefly Hopi and Navaho) to the supposed modes of thinking of their speakers. He contrasted these with the structures of English and other European languages, which he lumped together as Standard Average European (SAE), and the thinking manifested by these.

In 1954 a special conference was organized under the direction of Harry Hoijer to discuss Whorf's ideas (Hoijer 1954). At this meeting leading linguists found themselves thrusting in thin air, as anyone can see by reading the lengthy discussion (and Weinreich's perceptive review 1955). Whorf's works were diligently quoted in the writings of the disciples of Korzybski, founder of the "General Semantics" movement, e.g. S. I. Hayakawa and Dorothy Lee. A major test of these ideas was launched by John Carroll, with inconclusive results (Hymes and Bittle 1967).

It was Whorf's merit to take ideas that had been part of many linguists' stock-in-trade and try them out on the languages of the American Southwest. His eloquence and enthusiasm were infectious enough to excite a number of linguists with anthropological interests, as well as a wide circle of laymen. In this paper we shall examine some of the pitfalls of Whorf's thesis, sketching in some of his motivation and background.

In a comparative study of Shawnee and English, Whorf (1941, reprinted
in ed. by Carroll 1956) provides two English sentences which (he claims)
have nothing in common but the present tense and the subject pronoun "I":

(a) I pull the branch aside

(b) I have an extra toe on my foot

Then he produces Shawnee translations of these and finds that they are
"closely similar; in fact, they differ only at the tail end":

(c) ni-l'θawa-'ko-n-a

(d) ni-l'θawa-'ko-θite

"Shawnee logicians and observers would class the two phenomena as intrin-
sically similar." Whorf offers no informant's word for this statement, and he
presumably found no logicians to discuss it with. The opinion is based purely
on the surface similarity of the two sentences. We are justified in asking
just how valid his analysis is.

Basing our inquiry only on the information Whorf provides, the sentences
can be analysed morpheme-by-morpheme as:

(e) I-fork-tree-by hand-cause

(f) I-fork-tree-on toes-[have]

Sentence (c) is transitive, with "fork-tree" as the object of a movement
by the hand as instrument. Sentence (d) is possessive, with "fork-tree"
attributed to the toes as locative. Actually, the only common element in the
two Shawnee sentences is the phrase *l'θawa-'ko*. Whorf claims that *l'θawa*
is a common term denoting "a forked outline" and that -*'ko* may be a form
of a word denoting "tree, bush, tree part, branch, or anything of that general
shape." Whatever analysis one may make of its parts, the meaning of the
sentences offered shows that *l'θawa-'ko* need mean nothing more than
"branch," used in sentence (c) in a concrete sense and in sentence (d) in a
figurative sense.

Their similarity is somewhat less remarkable if we translate (c) as "I move
a branch with my hand," and (d) as "I have a branch on my foot." The
probability is infinitesimal that any considerable number of Shawnee had
extra toes on their feet. It is clear that sentence (d) was made up either to
illustrate Whorf's point or as a nonce and humorous way of referring to a
highly occasional deformity. It is no more than an illustration of the way
human imagination can and does see similarities between otherwise different
situations. It is no more surprising or expressive of any special quality of
Shawnee or the Shawnee mind than the fact that English "branch" can refer
to rivers, pipes, roads, antlers, families, languages, academic fields of study,
the houses of Congress, or business establishments, to mention only a few.
The striking difference between (a) and (b) is no more than an artifact of
his translation-interpretation.

Another of Whorf's examples in the same article illustrates the opposite situation, close similarity in English corresponding to startling dissimilarity in an Indian language, this time Nootka. Here sentences (a) and (b) are:

(a) The boat is grounded on the beach

(b) The boat is manned by picked men

Whorf analyzes these grammatically as "The boat is *x*ed preposition *y*," and hence linguistically and logically identical. Today it would be seen that there is a great difference in the deep structure between these sentences. Even then it should have been evident that the two prepositional phrases stood in wholly different relationships to the verbs. "On the beach" is a locative with a participial adjective, while "by picked men" is the logical subject of a passive verb.

The Nootka equivalents provided are:

(c) Tlih-is-ma

(d) Lash-tskwiq-ista-ma

Here the only common element means "third person indicative." Whorf's main point is that neither sentence contains a word for "boat". But there is in each of them a word that suggests activity connected with a boat (or rather, a canoe). In (c) this is *tlih-*, glossed as "moving pointwise," i.e. "traveling in or as a canoe." No evidence is given to show that the highly abstract gloss "moving pointwise" is a valid meaning; one naturally asks from what actual situations this has been abstracted.

Whorf compares the word to a "vector in physics" rather than a "thing." But the movement of a boat is not a "thing" in English either, and since the modifier *-is-* means "on the beach," the meaning here can hardly be one of pure motion. In English we have a phrase "to be headed" (in a certain direction), which could also be glossed as "moving pointwise"; but here the metaphor is based on the human head as a director of motion and hence the leading part, for instance of a boat. We can therefore gloss the morphemes of sentence (c) as "boat headed-on the beach-[there] is," with more likelihood of having identified the correct analysis underlying the interpretation "the boat is grounded on the beach."

In sentence (d) the morpheme implying the presence of a boat is *-ista-*, glossed as "in a canoe as crew." The form may be a locative adverbial, as suggested by the gloss, but its analysis of reality is not very different from our phrase "boat crew." It is modified by *lash-tskwiq-*, which is glossed as "selected" (literally "select, pick" plus "remainder, result"). The whole sentence may then be glossed as "select-ed-boat crew-[there] is," which is a step earlier in the translation process than either of Whorf's literal interpretations, "they are in the boat as a crew of picked men" and "the boat has a crew of picked men." And it is quite different from his free interpretation, which makes use of the peculiarly English verb "to man": "The boat is manned by picked men."

At best these sentences confirm the well-established fact that different cultures talk about different things in nature and have applied different analogies in expanding their vocabularies from the concrete to the abstract (or vice versa). These are interesting and important features in the relation of man to his culture and to his use of language within that culture. But they do not justify any judgments concerning a qualitative difference in the way men think. Similar discrepancies between the way languages partition nature are not limited to such major gaps as those between Hopi and what Whorf somewhat patronizingly called "Standard Average European." Such differences have been studied for French and German in attempts to derive some kind of "soul" characterization of the respective peoples. Anyone who works with the translation of texts from one language to another knows how often even closely related languages require fudging.

Whorf's strongest claims relate to the influence of the categories of grammar, i.e. the least conscious parts of the language. For English (and SAE) these include such categories as number, gender, and tense. The very fact that these are obligatory categories deprives them of any great informational value (Weinreich 1955). The speaker has no choice but to observe them as conventions implanted in the language. If they reflect any view concerning reality, it is at best one that was held by our presumably "primitive" Indo-European-speaking ancestors.

Only an incredible nalveté could suggest that the use of plurals has required us to develop or to function in a world of numbers and measurement, that the use of the tense forms has led us to keep records and develop what Whorf calls "historicity," or that the Hopi system of noun classification (which is analogical to our gender) required the Hopi to pay more attention to form and shape than other people. In the Southwest Project Hopi and American children were tested for their classification of objects by shape. The experiment failed, no doubt because the capacity of distinguishing and classifying objects by form is surely universally human. (Maclay 1958).

The real test comes when abstracts that have no shape or form are classified. Gender classification is simple in dealing with animate sex-marked beings. But when this is extended to inanimate and nonmaterial concepts, there is nothing compelling about it. In Latin the sun is masculine, the moon femine; in Scandinavian it is the other way around. English speakers, who have a gender system only in the pronouns, would be hard put to establish the probable gender in languages that retain gender distinctions.

Whorf makes much of the fact that the plural has a different range of application in Hopi and English, especially in relation to mass nouns (1939, in Carroll 1956: 140-141). But there are similar problems in SAE languages. Whorf writes of Hopi that "water" does not mean "the substance water", but one certain mass or quantity of water. In Norwegian *vann/vatn* means "water," but *et vann/vatn* means "a lake." Similarly *et brød* is "a loaf of bread," etc. Such data do not compel a philosophic distinction between "form" and "content."

Grammatical plurality only tells us that there is a difference between *one* and *more than one* (or *two*, in languages with a dual), hardly enough to make an important mathematical distinction. In Indo-European it is an obligatory distinction that clarifies the relation between subject and verb, nothing more.

Whorf is even more concerned with differences in the tense systems (1939, in Carroll 1956: 143-145). The "three-tense system" of past, present, and future "colors all our thinking about time." In fact, English has no simple future tense; perhaps he confuses tense with time. These are lexical devices, and future events are as often in the present ("I'm eating at six this evening") or the past ("If I told her . . ."). A simplistic view lays out the tenses in a straight line from left to right, but a phrase like "he laughed" only tells us that the action took place before the moment of speaking — a second or a million years ago.

A language may very well need adverbs to express such ideas, but one can hardly imagine a language that does not somehow convey the idea of past or futurity. According to Whorf, Hopi does not objectify time: "Nothing is suggested about time except the perpetual 'getting later' of it" (1941, in Carroll 1956: 143). More specific time indicators surely exist in Hopi, as they do in English. In Old Norse there are verbs like *sumra* "to become summer" etc.

Even if we sum up all the marked differences in grammatical structure between Hopi and English, they scarcely support his contention that "they point toward possible new types of logic and possible cosmical pictures" (1941, in Carroll 1956: 241). The idea that bipartite Greek logic arose from the bipartite Greek sentence has often enough been asserted. But the formalization of logic and mathematics is rather a rejection of the often illogical, if convenient, formulations of natural language. Mathematics may be seen as an attempt to overcome the inadequacies of natural language for the purpose of exact and elegant statement.

It therefore seems absurd when Whorf maintains that "modern Chinese or Turkish scientists . . . have taken over bodily the entire Western system of rationalizations" instead of corroborating it "from their native posts of observation." (1940, in Carroll 1956: 214). But there is nothing in English as such that enables us to talk about relativity or atomic energy or the double helix. In comparison with mathematics even the English terminology requires some distortion of the ideas involved.

When he maintains that the "formulation of ideas" is not strictly rational, "but is part of a particular grammar," he is guilty of begging the question.

We do not know, except by introspection (which is faulty) and by speculation (which is airy) just how ideas are formulated. He may be right in attacking a "rational" formulation, for ideas do come in extralinguistic form, as images, patterns, relationships, flashes of illumination. But language is eventually involved, for they are not communicable until they are formulated in a particular language and organized into the proper syntactic, lexical, and phonological patterns imposed by that language.

In Whorf's statement the "grammar" stands for the whole language, but many meanings that we wish to convey are not conveyed by the grammar at all. If my shepherd comes running to tell me that a wolf has eaten my sheep, there are three basic facts to be conveyed, which require a common vocabulary and a common grammar: "wolf", "eat," and "sheep." If he has the time, he may fit them into an empty scheme: NP_1 (actor) − V (action) − NP_2 (goal). But he need only cry "wolf!"

Divergent languages have different ways of expressing such sets of data, but all languages have ways of marking the basic relations, even if they differ widely in the way they apply them to reality. I therefore contend that the grammatical system as such has only a minimal connection with any formulation of ideas. The obligatory forms, like present − past or singular − plural or indefinite − definite, are mostly redundant, and they can be expressed lexically in languages where they are optional.

We shall look at possible approaches in our next chapter.

Chapter 22

Bilingual Judgments

Whorf's one-sided view of the language-thought relationship was not original with him. The general disregard of European linguistic thought by many American linguists in the 1940's kept them from realizing that these views had been debated by European linguists for some two centuries.

Roger Brown (1967) found that the men of the Enlightenment were inclined to think of reason as prior to language, making language a mere vehicle of thought. Their mutual dependence was suggested by a prize topic announced in 1757 by the Berlin Academy: "The influence of opinions on the language and of language on opinions" (Christmann 1967: 463). The essay that won the prize in 1759 by David Michaelis treated both sides of the problem in detail, especially the latter part of it, in terms that proved to have the greatest influence.

Coincident with and as a part of the development of literary Romanticism, the emphasis shifted towards the priority of language over thinking. Wilhelm von Humboldt went so far as to set up language as the independent variable: "Language is the formative organ of thought." "Every language sets certain limits to the spirit of those who speak it; it assumes a certain direction and, by doing so, excludes many others" (Brown 1967: 68, 84).

The idea was most forcefully expressed by Vico in Italy. He was followed by such Germans as Hamann, Herder, Fichte, and von Humboldt (Christmann 1967). These were countries that were divided and whose languages were oppressed. The thesis of linguistic determinism became, in effect, a weapon in the hands of nationalistic self-assertion. Herder proclaimed that "every nation has its own treasury of such ideas as have become symbols, ideas which are its national language: a treasury to which the nation has contributed for centuries . . . the intellectual treasury of an entire people" (Christmann 1967: 467).

Hamann declared that "every language requires a mode of thought that is peculiar to it". Von Humboldt carried the idea to the point of declaring: ". . . So there lies in every language a particular world view (*Weltansicht*). (Christmann 1967: 445). This idea was particularly welcome as an ideological base for the teaching and cultivation of the native language and the throwing off of classical and French influence. In modern times the idea was picked up and endlessly varied by the German scholar Leo Weisgerber, whose writings were influential in implanting in German textbooks the idea that "man comprehends and organizes physical and spiritual reality through his mother tongue" (Basilius 1952, Note 18 speaks of his "cultish" terminology).

By contrast, the Swedish linguist, Esaias Tegnér, presented a more balanced view in his *Språkets makt över tanken* (1880) (The power of language over thought). After discussing numerous examples from his native language of the kind of intellectual confusions that could be induced by natural languages, Tegnér rejected all attempts to correlate "national psychology" with features of the grammatical structure, e.g. Lepsius' contention that languages with a gender distinction reflected a more elevated moral conception of sex roles in family life! He did not deny that "grammatical features might exist that exerted an influence on the conceptualization of speakers" (Tegnér 1922: 242). But he exemplified this with the elaborate Swedish forms of address, which are rather lexical than grammatical: They have caused "many, not just social occasions, but also social affairs in a wider sense, to develop differently than they otherwise could and should have done." (Ibid. 264-265).

The line of descent from the German cult of linguistic relativity practised by von Humboldt and his followers, especially Max Müller, to the work of Whorf is clear and unbroken (Christmann 1967). Boas was German by birth and training and was familiar with this line of thinking. In his well-known introduction to the *Handbook of American Indian Languages* (1911), he devoted some lines to the problem: "It is commonly assumed that the linguistic expression is a secondary reflex of the customs of the people; but the question is quite open in how far the one phenomenon is the primary one and the other the secondary one, and whether the customs of the people have not rather developed from the unconsciously developed terminology" (Boas 1966: 69). While he denied that "a certain state of culture is conditioned by morphological traits of the language," he was willing to believe that the metaphorical use of certain terms might have led to the rise of certain views or customs. These ideas were well calculated to lead up to his emphasis on language study "as one of the most important branches of ethnological study," not just for its practical value, but also because "the peculiar characteristics of languages are clearly reflected in the views and customs of the peoples of the world."

Sapir, a student of Boas', is often credited with formulating the relativity hypothesis, but Sapir vacillated on this point, as Hymes has pointed out (1964: 118-119, 128). In *Language* (1921: 234) he denied any correlation between language form and cultural content: "When it comes to linguistic form, Plato walks with the Macedonian swineherd, Confucius with the head-hunting savage of Assam." But in a later article he was concerned with demonstrating the value of linguistics "as a science," and he formulated the power of language over thought: "The fact of the matter is that the 'real world' is to a large extent unconsciously built up on the language habits of the group" (1929: 209). His examples are all lexical and leave it open to question just what he meant by "language habits". But it should not be overlooked that these phrases were part of a special plea for the importance of linguistics.

Whorf's views, at least partly shaped by Sapir, bear a similar impress of enthusiastic advocacy. In a study of the tenses of Chichewa, an East African language, Whorf concluded: "It may be that these primitive folk are equipped with a language which, if they were to become philosophers or mathematicians, could make them our foremost thinkers.upon *time*" (1942, in Carroll 1956: 266). The fact that Hopi discriminates three kinds of conjunctions all translated "that" in English convinced him that the "formal systematization of ideas" in English, German, French, or Italian was "poor and jejune" compared with that of Hopi: "English compared to Hopi is like a bludgeon compared to a rapier" (Carroll 1956: 85).

In his articles printed in the M. I. T. *Technology Review*, Whorf made it a point to rehabilitate "the province of the despised grammarian" (1940, in Carroll 1956: 211). He wanted to show his natural scientist readers "the incredible degree of diversity of linguistic systems that ranges over the globe" and so "foster that humility which accompanies the true scientific spirit." The study of Hopi and other Indian languages would prevent us from regarding "a few recent dialects of the Indo-European family, and the rationalizing techniques elaborated from their patterns, as the apex of the evolution of the human mind." (1940, in Carroll 1956: 218).

One is reminded that Whorf came to linguistics with a mystic point of view which colors even his most scientific work. In Carroll's biographical sketch we learn that Whorf studied Hebrew because he believed that "fundamental human and philosophical problems could be solved by taking a new sounding of the semantics of the Bible" (but see Barr 1961). An early enthusiasm for the French linguistic mystic Fabre d'Olivet was replaced by Sapir's teachings after 1928. But the study of Hopi that followed was inspired by a conviction that "the Hopi actually have a language better equipped to deal with . . . vibratile phenomena than is our latest scientific terminology" (1936, in Carroll 1956: 55).

Whorf's last major article and many minor ones appeared in a theosophical journal published at Madras, India. In one of these he called for an appreciation of "the types of logical thinking which are reflected in truly Eastern forms of scientific thought or analysis of nature. This requires linguistic research into the logics of native languages and realization that they have equal scientific validity with our thinking habits" (Carroll 1956: 21). In "Language, Mind, and Reality" (1941) he found in "the scientific understanding of very diverse languages . . . a lesson in brotherhood which is brotherhood in the universal human principle" (1941, in Carroll 1956: 263). He went on: "The Algonkian languages are spoken by very simple people, hunting and fishing Indians, but they are marvels of analysis and synthesis." For him linguistic research became part of the path to Yoga, with a "therapeutic value" to free patients from "the compulsive working over and over of word systems".

We may find Whorf's goals sympathetic, but his immersion in these ideas left many of his results in the state of being little more than cultish hypotheses. Much of the interest that his advocacy of the relativity hypothesis aroused was a result of an emotional commitment on the part of anthropological linguists. They were all in the position of needing to justify the effort expended on the study of American Indian languages. They needed better grounds than the mere accumulation of knowledge. They had to contend that language was not just a mirror, but also an essential factor in shaping human culture. Whorf offered linguists the exciting prospect of making their discipline an "exact science," the title of one of his essays.

In discussing the theory of linguistic relativity we have hopefully succeeded in showing that it is most congenial to the romantic thinker, while universalism appeals most to the rationalist thinker. But we have not thereby established a truth value for either.

It is worth considering that bilinguals might be the best resource for the study of this problem. They alone can personally testify to the differential effect of the "world view" imposed by different languages since they have experience with monolingual speakers of each language. On this point there is some limited evidence.

The anthropologist Robert H. Lowie recounted his experience as an Austrian immigrant to the United States at the age of ten (Lowie 1945; 258). He tried to maintain his German as he learned English, noting both the difficulties and the insights that resulted. "The popular impression that a man alters his personality when speaking another tongue is far from ill-grounded. When I speak German to Germans, I automatically shift my orientation as a social being. I spontaneously adapt myself to the atmosphere characteristic of their status, outlook, prejudices. The very use of the customary formulae of politeness injects a distinct flavor into the conversation, coloring attitudes and behavior. Some of these modes of expression, to be sure, are merely meaningless formulae, but by no means all." He refers to the use of titles which contrasts with the "free and easy" American way of dropping them. "Language is so intimately interwoven with the whole of social behavior that a bilingual, for better or worse, is bound to differ from the monoglot."

The French-born American writer, Julian Green, wrote about the problems involved in writing books in two languages. He found that it was impossible for him to translate one of his books from French into English. He had to sit down and write an entirely new book: "It was as if, writing in English, I had become another person." (Green 1941: 402).

The German-Italian bilingual linguist Theodor W. Elwert explored in detail his own problems of social and personal adjustment to a succession of early language-learning experiences. He rejected Lowie's formulation: "On changing languages, we do not change our character [Wesen], but our attitude [Verhalten] ... In principle, the process is the same as in changing from one setting [Milieu] to another of the same language.... We do not change our behavior (and even less our personality) because we change language, but we change language because we have to change our behavior in a new setting ... Language is only a part of a larger behavioral complex" (Elwert 1960: 344, fn. 1).

It becomes evident from these and other accounts that the learning of a second language requires adjustment to the ways of speaking and behaving that are customary in the new group. This adjustment leaves the bilingual with a keen sense of the difficulty in keeping two languages and the corresponding cultures apart. Lowie gives many valuable examples of his own problems in maintaining equal adequacy in both languages.

Because none of the three people here mentioned discusses possible experiences with non-Indo-European languages (though Lowie knew Crow, as Ives Goddard has pointed out to me), their observations may be considered inadequate, in view of the claims made by Whorf. But there is no reason to believe that other memoirs or self-reports would reveal anything different. Thinking in one language is different from thinking in another, but it is reasonably clear that this is largely a matter of vocabulary. One thinks most readily in each language about those topics that one has learned the vocabulary for in that language. Most bilinguals whom I have consulted on this problem have denied that they felt like a "different person" in speaking their other language.

From my own experience I can confirm the views of Elwert. One does not become a different person or think differently in another language that one feels as an intimate part of one's experience. One is glad to act as a fully accepted member of the speech community, and as such one does adopt a different set of expectations. In formulating some ideas one may feel that one language facilitates the formulation while another forces a rather different formulation. Each language has its shortcuts and its circumlocutions. These have little to do with the grammar in the usual sense: phonology, morphology, syntax.

Norwegian morphology requires that the definite article be suffixed on nouns, but preposed before adjectives: *huset* "the house", *det hvite* "the white" (one). If the phrase includes both adjective and noun, there is a choice. In daily life one uses both: *det hvite huset* "the white house." But in formal (and old-fashioned) style the second article can be deleted: *Det hvite hus* "the White House". This complex rule of Norwegian style contrasts with the simple English "the." A rule of syntax governs the use of the article to replace possessives: *han mistet hatten* "he lost the [i.e. his] hat." A lexical rule requires the article with abstracts (which is rare in English but known from French and German): *kjærligheten* "[the] love", *kunsten* "[the] art." These (and a host of more detailed rules) require learning and can produce interferences for bilingual speakers.

So one has a more than adequate basis for paraphrasing Whorf's statement about the Hopi plural: the definite article is not the same in Norwegian as in English, whether phonologically, morphologically, or semantically. But there is no warrant for claiming that for this reason Norwegians "think" differently from Americans. The definite article is not a philosophical concept, however difficult grammarians may find it to formulate rules for its precise use in one or several languages. Among other things, it is a mechanical device for marking identity of reference in a sequence of noun phrases. It is especially useful in languages like English and Norwegian, which lack case endings. For one's "world view" it has as much significance as does the mortar that joins the bricks in a wall for the thinking of those who live within.

Macnamara has reduced the cognitive problem to absurdity by describing the bilingual's dilemma if Whorf's idea should be true (Macnamara 1970: 25-40). Either he uses Language$_1$ or Language$_2$ and is unable to understand the other, or he uses both and is unable to communicate with himself! The answer to this is, of course, that every speaker can interpret systems different from his own even if he cannot produce them. A bilingual simply interprets L$_1$ and L$_2$ for their intended meanings, and in many cases even forgets which language he learned them in. This suggests that there must be a store of knowledge in the mind that is relatively language-free. This may turn out to be the answer to Whorf's problem as well.

Chapter 23

Language Choice

> "...There are, perhaps, two main reasons
> why one should learn the language of
> another man: in order to trade with him,
> or to have power over him, religious or
> political."
>
> (W. Whiteley 1969: 55)

Bilinguals are by definition persons who have a choice between dialects or languages. In practice it is not uncommon that they choose to use one rather than the other. What are the reasons? Is there a rationale that one can identify? The topic is closely connected with the problems of minority languages and of what has come to be called "language death."

To my knowledge the first to suggest the importance of studying the fate of dying languages was Morris Swadesh, whose research on Native American languages had given him abundant opportunity to observe languages with only one or a few speakers. In an article on "obsolescent" languages he noted that "many of the circumstances described are similar to those found in the languages of some immigrant groups..." (Swadesh 1938, publ. 1948: 226; see also Elmendorf 1981). An early student of language choice was Simon R. Herman (1961), who described the vacillation of immigrants to Israel between English and Hebrew, due to differential reception. These observations could be amplified by my studies of American immigrant groups (Haugen 1953 etc.).

On looking back at my own choices, as they were outlined above (chapter 2), I realize that I was in some ways deviant, downright un-American. The home atmosphere of ethnic loyalty was basic, reinforced by my two happy years as a boy in Norway. Norwegian became an ethnic imperative, re-enforced by a variety of rewards. An observer might conclude that I was enabled to play the role of a big frog in a little pond. It has therefore puzzled me in later years to meet countrymen who refused to speak their mother tongue with me. I have asked myself: how can people become so anglicized that they reject what ought to be a welcome opportunity?

During my field work in Wisconsin and Minnesota I often asked the question and got some forthright answers. A woman who preferred Norwegian to English sermons added: "As things are in this country, people marry into other nationalities, and the children don't get taught Norwegian. So I suppose it's best that it's losing out, but I'll be sorry to see it go entirely." "I think it has to go that way," said one man: "we're in America, English is the language of the land..." Several commented on the influence of the public school. As one man put it, "When my boy was small, he spoke only Norwegian, but after starting school, he changed right over." (Haugen 1953a: 273).

The picture that emerged was one of a large number of individual choices, gradually turning whole communities over from one language to the other. In horse-and-buggy days the individual farm was more of a self-contained unit, with less American contact than later. What is often called "language loyalty" may in some cases be more like cultural isolation. This is certainly the explanation of the survival of German in Pennsylvania, of French in Quebec, and of the constantly immigrating Hispanics today.

In a spirit of resignation I was led to accept the idea of regarding the learning of languages as a transaction of commodities. In an immigrant community the mother tongue is a precious commodity as long as it preserves the individual's identity and offers a perspective of future well-being. Learning of language exacts its price from the learner, and he or she will resist paying the price unless the benefits it brings are commensurate with the cost. (Haugen 1983)

Any language has its market value, which like those of all other commodities, fluctuates with the market. The market in question may be called a *language market*, which determines the values that an individual or a society attaches to each language. Happily the market value is not only or even necessarily monetary, although that is surely important. In an immigrant group where most members are dependent on the majority society for jobs, facility in the majority language is essential.

It need not be an immigrant community. Nancy C. Dorian (1981) has chronicled the story of the decline of Gaelic in east Sutherland in northern Scotland. In part the tale goes back to a desire by landowners to introduce sheepgrazing in order to gain greater profits from the Scottish highland. The crofters who had their homes there were evicted and removed to the coast. Here they were expected to learn fishing, a trade for which they were quite unprepared. They became a fishing proletariat in the coastal villages, purveyors of cheap food, looked down upon and socially segregated.

These fishermen proved to be the most retentive of Gaelic, since they were isolated from their fellow townsmen during the general turn-over of the Scottish people from Gaelic to (Scots) English. Dorian does not dignify it by calling it "language loyalty"; she terms it "linguistic lag."

She notes that in 1500 Gaelic speech was virtually universal in Scotland. But thanks to a small anglified upper class, the language that had been Scotland's, was gradually stigmatized. It became "lower class," and as it retreated into the Highlands, the language of a wild, barbarous people. Dorian is sympathetic to the plight of her informants and denies that the result is inevitable (p. 72, 111). But her careful and lively account brings to light social trends and human weaknesses that come as close as possible to making "language death" inevitable.

Anyone who did not wish to participate in the cycle from Gaelic to English was isolated, "queer," or even obstreperous, as we see from the punishments meted out to Gaelic-speaking children. This barbarous form of education was also known in American schools in immigrant communities. Even where the stick has been hidden behind the schoolroom door, the carrot that replaced it has had the same effect. The larger society has a plethora of inducements for the bright boy or girl, provided they are not linguistically deviant. Gaelic speech is a remediable "defect," a part of group identity that can be shed.

From Scotland we turn even farther afield, to East Africa. We are well instructed by Carol Scotton in her book on "choosing a Lingua Franca" in Kampala, the capital of Uganda (1972). Here the choice is three-way, between one of a multitude of local vernaculars; Swahili, the East African lingua franca; and English, the language of the former rulers. English is the only official language, contrary to neighboring Tanzania, where Swahili is official. A reason for the difference is that Uganda is predominantly Christian, while Swahili is traditionally associated with Mohammedanism.

Swahili has nevertheless had phenomenal success in spreading among the people, even in Uganda, as the language one uses to members of other tribes than one's own. Being a Bantu language, it is not hard to learn; Kampala even has a dialect of its own. Educated speakers are contemptuous, calling it the language of "prostitutes and swindlers." English is the language of the educated, since it is learned only in school, where it is the medium of secondary instruction. Within Uganda it "characterizes the everyday public dealings of the educated and successful African." (p. 26). But to use it with fellow workers is offensive, except as a switching technique.

The image of Swahili as a neutral language that implies nothing about one's ethnic or socioeconomic status was confirmed by Scotton's studies in Kenya (and of Pidgin English in Nigeria) (1976). These situations show that "neutral" ethnicity is a quality that adheres to these languages by contrast with the local vernaculars. The educated have the further option of using English as well, in some situations as a device of status-raising, in others of varying the social distance.

The trilingual situation in East Africa is not unlike my own situation. I have a three-way choice, arranged as two double dichotomies, and the African system can be similarly diagrammed:

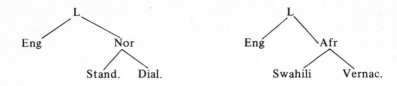

In speaking to a member of my own Norwegian dialect community I will use that dialect; it is the vernacular of my childhood and of my contacts with its speakers. Just so a Ugandan will speak his vernacular to members of his own tribe. To other Norwegians I will use standard (Dano-) Norwegian, i.e. Bokmål as a neutral language, but also to Swedes and Danes (as Ugandans communicate in Swahili with Tanzanians and Kenyans). There is even an interesting historical parallel in that my Norwegian has Danish as one of its ancestors, just as Swahili is imported from the coast into Uganda.

Among Norwegians in America, however, the choice between vernacular and standard existed only as long as sermons and parochial schools were held in Norwegian. Then and later the major choice was between an American-Norwegian vernacular and American English, corresponding to the African choice between Swahili and English and the Scottish one between Gaelic and English.

We should emphasize that in none of the situations of language choice are we speaking of an absolute either-or. Wherever possible there is a continuum, within which each speaker places him- or herself in relation to other speakers. In east Sutherland Dorian explicitly points to the constant switching of codes as well as extensive borrowing (transfers), chiefly from the more prestigious language into the lesser one. She has made a special study of so-called "semi-speakers" of Gaelic. They represent that fringe of passive bilinguals whose memories retain much of the grammar and lexicon, but not enough to qualify as proper speakers. Scotton also notes the frequency of switching from Swahili to English and the tendency of Swahili speakers to borrow from English.

In short, the situations described by these scholars correspond very closely with those that are well-known in American immigrant languages, as Swadesh foresaw. My dual bilingualism appears to have its parallels wherever languages meet under conditions of unequal extension or prestige. Minorities are dominated by elites, and languages are means by which elites maintain their dominion. They make the minorities uncertain of their own values, and they press or encourage them to reject their old ethnicities, without necessarily granting them admission to or status in the new society.

Scotton and Dorian are in a sense looking at language choice from opposite ends of the spectrum. Dorian is studying "language death," while Scotton may be said to be studying "language birth." Scotton has recorded the trend toward the adoption of what is essentially a foreign, though easily learned language, Swahili. Except where the population has been decimated, the "last" speaker is also a "first" speaker; what they have in common is language shift. The vernaculars could be threatened if English or Swahili should become, singly or jointly, permanent lingua francas in Uganda.

Dorian shows how the social isolation of the fisher folk is a factor in the maintenance of Gaelic (p. 102). Scotton shows how breakdown of isolation leads to shift. Both have found that innovations are emotionally charged: anyone who deviates by adopting the dominant language will "be viewed as something of a traitor to his original group" (Dorian, p. 103). In eastern Sutherland such people are described as "proud." One of Scotton's informants used the identical term: "People prefer using Swahili to avoid the suspicion that they use English because they are proud." (Scotton p. 120). The Norwegian-American terms for people who "anglify" are pejorative: they are either *engelsksprengt* ("English-bloated") or *jenkisprengt* ("Yankee-bloated"). (Haugen 1953: 476).

Both Dorian and Scotton account for some of their findings in terms of *value*. Dorian writes that "parents and children agreed on the positive value of English and the negative value of Gaelic for the rising generation" (p. 105). Scotton accepts Homans' theory of social behavior as an exchange (1958), harking back to Mauss' essay on the gift (1925). Thibaut and Kelley (1959) saw human relations "in terms of a balancing of costs and reward" (p. 102). Extending this to language, Scotton sees the choices made by weighing the relative costs and rewards (1972: 109; 1976).

In sum, there is a consensus that language choices leading either to the birth or death of languages are significant social decisions. They are based on the speakers' view of the respective values of the languages or dialects on the language market. These values, which ultimately involve the speaker's opportunities for living a good life as an accepted member of a community, will shift over time. In a relatively isolated community linguistic cohesion may lead to a loyalty that will prevent language shift.

Isolation may be either geographical or social. To the extent that a community is economically or politically dependent on the goodwill of another community with a different language, the value of its own language will fall. Those who are upwardly mobile will be tempted if not forced to change languages. Learning and maintaining a second language is costly in time and mental energy. But its values far exceed the cost if it broadens one's experience and enriches one's life.

Bibliography

A. Articles on which Chapters are Based

1 Babel — The Curse of Babel. *Dædalus*, Summer Issue 1973, 47-57.
2 On Growing Up Bilingual — Personal Reflections on Growing Up Bilingual. *Bilingualism and Bilingual Education: New Readings and Insights*, ed. J. Ornstein-Galicia and Robert St. Clair (Trinity University, 1979/80), 251-281.
3 Bilingual Competence — On the Meaning of Bilingual Competence. *Studies in General and Oriental Linguistics, Presented to Shiro Hattori*, ed. R. Jakobson and S. Kawamoto (Tokyo: TEC Company Ltd., 1970), 221-229. — Bilingualism as a Social and Personal Problem. *Active Methods and Modern Aids in the Teaching of Foreign Languages*, ed. R. Filipović (London: Oxford 1972), 1-14.
4 The Ethnic Imperative — Language and Ethnicity. *Lögberg-Heimskringla*, Dec. 4, 1975 (Winnipeg, Sask., Canada).
5 An Ecological Model — An Ecological Model for Bilingualism. *Notes on Linguistics* No. 12, 1979, 14-20.
6 The Communicative Norm — Norm and Deviation in Bilingual Communities. *Bilingualism: Psychological, Social and Educational Implications*, ed. Peter A. Hornby (NY, Academic Press, 1977), 91-102. — Language Norms in Bilingual Communities. *Proceedings of the 12. Int. Congress of Linguists* (Vienna, Aug. 28-Sept. 2, 1977), ed. W. Dressler and W. Meid (Innsbruck 1978), 283-286.
7 Social Integration — Immigrant Language as an Index of Social Integration. *Scando-American Papers on Scandinavian Emigration to the United States*, ed. I. Semmingsen and P. Seyersted (Oslo: American Institute, 1980), 182-201.
8 Sociolinguistics: A Challenge — Some Issues in Sociolinguistics. *Issues in Sociolinguistics*, ed. O. Uribe-Villagas (The Hague: Mouton, 1977), 113-144. — The Challenge of Sociolinguistics. *The Nordic Languages and Modern Linguistics* 3, ed. J. Weinstock (Austin, Texas: The University of Texas, 1978), 3-9.
9 Pluralism: a National Goal? — Linguistic Pluralism as a Goal of National Policy. *Language and Society*, ed. Douglas C. Walker (Ottawa: Université d'Ottawa, 1977), 66-82.
10 Language Planning — Language Problems and Language Planning. The Scandinavian Model. *Sprachkontakt und Sprachkonflikt*, ed. Peter Hans Nelde (Heft 32, *Zeitschrift f. Dialektologie und Linguistik*, 1980), 151-157.
11 Implementation — The Implementation of Corpus Planning. *Progress in*

Language Planning, ed. J. Cobarrubias and J. Fishman (Berlin etc., Mouton, 1983), 269-289.

12 Semicommunication — Language Fragmentation in Scandinavia: Revolt of the Minorities. *Minority Languages Today*, ed. E. Haugen, J.D. McClure, D.S. Thomson (Edinburgh Univ. Press, 1981), 100-119.

13 Interlanguage — Skandinavisk som mellomspråk. *Forskning og fremtid. Internordisk språkförståelse*, ed. Claes-Christian Elert (Umeå, Sweden: *Acta* 33, 1981), 121-143.

14 English: Modernization — The English Language as an Instrument of Modernization in Scandinavia. *Det moderna Skandinaviens framväxt* (Uppsala: *Acta Universitatis, Symposium* 10, 1978), 81-91.

15 Faroese: Ecology — Language Ecology and the Case of Faroese. *Linguistic Method: Essays in Honor of Herbert Penzl*, ed. I. Rauch and G.E. Carr (The Hague: Mouton, 1979), 183-197. [Also in *Linguistic and Literary Studies in Honor of Arhibald A. Hill*, ed. M. Jazayery, E.C. Polomé, and W. Winter, vol. 4 (The Hague: Mouton, 1979), 243-257.

16 Icelandic: Pronominal Address — Pronominal Address in Icelandic: From You-two to You-all. *Language in Society* 4.323-339 (1975)

17 Norwegian: Forms of Address — Norwegian Forms of Address. *Studia Linguistica* 32. 91-96, 1978.

18 Norwegian: Sexism. — "Sexism" and the Norwegian Language. *Studies in Descriptive and Historical Linguistics: Festschrift for Winfred P. Lehmann*, ed. Paul J. Hopper (Amsterdam, Benjamins, 1977), 83-94.

19 Norwegian: A Frontier — Frontier Norwegian in South Dakota. *Languages in Conflict: Linguistic Acculturation on the Great Plains*, ed. Paul Schach (Lincoln: Univ. of Nebraska Press/Center for Great Plains Studies, 1980), 20-27.

20 Ethnicity: Swedes and Norwegians. — Svensker og nordmenn i Amerika: En studie i nordisk etnisitet. *Saga och sed* (K. Gustav Adolfs Akademiens *Årsbok*, 1976), 38-55.

21 Relativity — Linguistic Relativity: Myths and Methods. *Language and Thought: Anthropological Issues*, ed. Wm. C. McCormack and S.A. Wurm (The Hague: Mouton, 1977), 11-28.

22 Bilingual Judgments — Same as preceding.

23 Language Choice — The Rationale of Language Choice. *Proceedings of the 13th Intern. Congress of Linguists* August 29 — September 4, 1982, Tokyo. (Tokyo: CIPL, 1983), 317-328.

B. Books and Articles Referred To

Amundsen, S.S. and Reimund Kvideland. 1975. *Emigrantviser.* Oslo etc.: Universitetsforlaget.

Andersson, Theodore and Mildred Boyer. 1970. *Bilingual Schooling in the United States.* Austin, Tex.: Southwest Educational Development Laboratory. 2 v.

Andersson, Thorsten. 1976. "Manlig sjuksköterska." *Nordiska Studier i filologi och lingvistik* (Festskrift tillägnad Gösta Holm), Lund), 1-11.
Arsenian, Seth. 1937. *Blingualism and Mental Deveopment*. New York: Teachers College, Columbia University.
Bandle, Oskar. 1979. "Soziolinguistische Strukturen in den nordischen Sprachen." *Standard und Dialekt* (Bern: Francke Verlag), 217-238.
Bang, Jørgen. 1962. *Om at bruge fremmedord*. Copenhagen: Schultz.
Barr, James. 1961. *The Semantics of Biblical Language*. London: Oxford.
Basilius, Harold. 1952. "Neo-Humboldtian Ethno-linguistics." *Word* 8.95-105.
Bernstein, Basil. 1962. "Social Class, Linguistic Codes, and Grammatical Elements." *Language and Speech* 5. 221-240.
—. 1971. *Class, Codes and Control*, v. 1. London: Routledge and Kegan Paul.
Berry, J.W. 1974. "Psychological Aspects of Cultural Pluralism: Unity and Identity Reconsidered." *Topics in Culture Learning* (Honolulu, Hawaii: East-West Center) 2. 17-22.
Bessason, Haraldur. 1967. "A Few Specimens of North-American Icelandic." *Scandinavian Studies* 39. 115-146.
—. 1971. "Isländskan i Nordamerika." *Språk i Norden 1971* (Oslo: Norsk språknemnd), 57-77.
Blakar, Rolf. 1973. *Språk er makt*. Oslo: Pax Forlag.
Blalock, Hubert M., Jr. 1967. *Toward a Theory of Minority-group Relations*. New York: Wiley.
Blaubergs, Maija S. 1978a. "Changing the Sexist Language: the Theory Behind the Practice." *Psychology of Women Quarterly* 2. 244-261.
—. 1978b. "Sociolinguistic Change Towards Nonsexist Language: an Overview and Analysis of Misunderstandings and Misapplications." Paper given at 9. World Congress of Sociology, Uppsala, Sweden.
Bloomfield, Leonard. 1933. *Language*. New York: Holt.
Boas, Franz. 1911. "Introduction," *Handbook of American Indian Languages* [Repr. ed. by Preston Holder, 1966, Lincoln: University of Nebraska Press].
Borgen, Johan. 1972. *Min arm min tarm*. Oslo: Gyldendal.
Bothne, Thrond. 1889. *Udsigt over det lutherske Kirkearbeide blandt Nordmændene i Amerika*. Chicago.
Braun, Maximilian. 1937. "Beobachtungen zur Frage der Mehrsprachigkeit." *Göttingische Gelehrte Anzeigen* 119. 115-130.
Braunmüller, Kurt. 1979. "Mehrsprachigkeit, Diglossie und Sprachprobleme in Skandinavien." *Current Issues in Linguistic Theory*, ed. B. Brogyanyi (Amsterdam Studies in Linguistic Science IV), 11. 139-157.
Brems, Hans. 1979. "The Collapse of the Binational Danish Monarchy in 1864: A Multinational Perspective." *Scandinavian Studies* 51. 428-441.
Bright, William, ed. 1966. *Sociolinguistics: Proceedings of the UCLA Sociolinguistics Conference, 1964*. The Hague: Mouton.
Bright, William and A.K. Ramanujan. 1964. "Sociolinguistic Variation and Language Change." *Proceedings, 9. Intern. Congress of Linguists, Cambridge, Mass., August 27, 1962*, ed. Horace Lunt (The Hague: Mouton), 1107-1114.

Brown, Roger L. 1967. *Wilhelm von Humboldt's Conception of Linguistic Relativity*. The Hague: Mouton.
Brown, Roger, and Marguerite Ford. 1961. "Address in American English." *Jrnl. Amer. Psych. Assn.* 62. 375-385 [Repr. in Hymes 1964, 234-244].
Brown, Roger, and Albert Gilman. 1960. "The Pronouns of Power and Solidarity." *Style in Language*, ed. T. Sebeok (Cambridge, Mass.: M.I.T. Press), 253-276.
Brugmann, Karl. 1911. *Grundriss der vergleichenden Grammatik der indogermanischen Sprachen*. Vol. 2, Part 2. Strassburg: K.J. Trübner.
Bull, Edvard. 1922. "Administration og embedsmænd." *Kristianias Historie* (Oslo: Kristiania Kommune), 1. 239-244.
Canada: Royal Commission on Bilingualism and Bicultualism. 1965. *A Preliminary Report*. Ottawa.
Carlsson, Sten. 1970. *Skandinaviske politiker i Minnesota 1882-1900*. Uppsala: Acta Universitatis Upsaliensis (Folia Historica Upsaliensia I).
Carmichael, Stokely and Charles V. Hamilton. 1967. *Black Power*. New York: Random.
Carroll, John B. 1956. Cf. Whorf, Benjamin.
Casad, Eugene H. 1974. *Dialect Intelligibility Testing*. Norman, Oklahoma: Summer Institute of Linguistics (Publ. No. 38).
Chomsky, Noam. 1965. *Aspects of the Theory of Syntax*. Cambridge, Mass.: M.I.T. Press.
Christmann, Hans Helmut. 1967. *Beiträge zur Geshichte der These vom Weltbild der Sprache*. Akademie der Wissenschaften und der Literatur (Abhandlungen 1959, Nr. 6), Mainz.
Clark, Virginia P. (To appear). "Women and Language: Some Current Research."
Clausen, Sven. 1938f. [*Årbog for*] *Nordisk målstræv*. Copenhagen: Nyt Nordisk Forlag [Periodical 1938-1947].
Clausén, Ulla. 1978. *Nyord i färöiskan: Ett bidrag till belysning av språksituationen på Färöarna*. Stockholm: Stockholm Studies in Scandinavian Philology, 14.
Clyne, Michael G. 1967. *Transference and Triggering: Observations on the Language Assimilation of Postwar German-speaking Migrants in Australia*. The Hague: Nijhoff.
—. 1972. *Perspectives on Language Contact, Based on the Study of German-speaking Migrants in Australia*. The Hague: Nijhoff.
Cohen, Marcel. [1956.] *Pour une sociologie du langage*. Paris. Michel.
Currie, Haver C. 1952. "A Projection of Socio-Linguistics: The Relation of Speech to Social Status." *Southern Speech Journal* 18. 28-37. [Repr. in *A Various Language*, ed. Juanita V. Williamson and Virginia M. Burke (New York: Holt, Rinehart and Winston), 39-47].
Dahlstedt, Karl-Hampus, Gösta Bergman, and Carl Ivar Ståhle. 1962. *Främmande ord i nusvenskan*. Stockholm: Verdandis skriftserie 17.
Décsy, G. 1973. *Die linguistische Struktur Europas*. Wiesbaden: Harrassowitz.
De Simone, Daniel V. 1971. *A Metric America: A Decision Whose Time has*

Come. Washington, D.C.: Superintendent of Documents (Special Publication, National Bureau of Standards, 345).

Deutsch, Karl W. 1953. *Nationalism and Social Communication.* Cambridge, Mass.: M.I.T. Press.

Diebold, Richard. 1961. "Incipient Bilingualism." *Language* 37. 97-112 [Repr. in Hymes 1964, 495-508].

Diller, Karl C. 1970/2 (1973). "'Compound' and 'Coordinate' Bilingualism – a Conceptual Artifact." *Word* 1970/2, 254-261.

Djupedal, Reidar. 1964. "Litt om framvoksteren av det færøyske skriftmålet." *Skriftspråk i utvikling* (Oslo: Norsk språknemnd), 144-186.

Dorfman, Joseph. 1934. *Thorstein Veblen and his America.* New York: Viking Press.

Dorian, Nancy C. 1981. *Language Death: The Life Cycle of a Scottish Gaelic Dialect.* Philadelphia: Univ. of Pennsylvania Press.

Elert, Claes, ed. 1981. *Internordisk språkförståelse.* Umeå: Umeå Studies in the Humanities, 33.

Elmendorf, William W. 1981. "Last Speakers and Language Change: Two California Cases." *Anthropological Linguistics,* January, 32-49.

Elwert, W. Theodor. 1960. *Das zweisprachige Individuum: Ein Selbstzeugnis.* Mainz: Akademie der Wissenschaften und der Literatur (Abh. der Geistes- und Socialwiss. Kl., Jahrg. 1959, Nr. 6).

Enninger, Werner and Lilith M. Haynes, eds. 1984. *Studies in Language Ecology.* Beiheft 43, *Zeitschr. f. Dialektologie und Linguistik* (herausg. J. Göschel).

Ervin-Tripp, Susan. 1967. "An Issei Learns English." *Journal of Social Issues* 23. 78-90.

Ferguson, Charles. 1959. "Diglossia." *Word* 15. 325-340. [Repr. in Hymes 1964, 429-439].

—. 1968. "Language Development." *Language Problems of Developing Nations,* ed. J. Fishman, C. Ferguson, J. Das Gupta (New York: Wiley), 27-36.

—. 1971. *Language Structures and Language Use.* Essays. Selected and Introduced by Anwar Dil. Stanford, Cal.: Stanford University Press.

Ferguson, Charles and John Gumperz, eds. 1960. *Linguistic Diversity in South Asia: Studies in Regional, Social and Functional Variation. Intern. Journal of Amer. Linguistics* 26. 3.

Finkenstaedt, T. 1963. *You and Thou: Studien zur Anrede im Englischen.* Berlin (Quellen und Forschungen, n. f. 10).

Fishman, Joshua A. 1965a. "Who Speaks What Language to Whom and When?" *La linguistique* 2. 67-88.

—. 1965b. "Varieties of Ethnicity and Varieties of Language Consciousness." *Georgetown University Monograph Series 18* (Washington, D.C.), 69-79.

—. 1966a. *Language Loyalty in the United States.* The Hague: Mouton.

—. 1966b. *Hungarian Language Maintenance in the United States.* Bloomington, Ind.: Indiana University Press (Uralic and Altaic Series 62).

—. 1967. "Bilingualism With and Without Diglossia: Diglossia With and Without Bilingualism." *Journal of Social Issues* 23. 29-38.

—. ed. 1968. *Readings in the Sociology of Language*. The Hague: Mouton.

—. ed. 1971. *Advances in the Sociology of Language*, vol. 1. The Hague: Mouton.

—. ed. 1974a. *Advances in Language Planning*. The Hague: Mouton.

—. 1974b. *A Sociology of Bilingual Education*. Stenciled: Final Report for U.S. Office of Education.

Fleming, Patricia. 1979. Article in the *Boston Globe*, February 27.

Fowler, H.W. 1926. *Dictionary of Modern English Usage*. London: Oxford University Press (Revised ed. by Ernest Gowers 1965).

Friedrich, Paul. 1966. "Structural Implications of Russian Pronominal Usage." *Sociolinguistics*, ed. W. Bright (New York: Wiley), 214-259.

Gal, Susan. 1979. *Language Shift: Social Determinants of Linguistic Change in Bilingual Austria*. New York: Academic Press (Language, Thought and Culture).

Garvin, Paul. 1973. "Some Comments on Language Planning." *Language Planning: Current Issues and Research*, ed. J. Rubin and R. Shuy (Washington, D.C.: Georgetown University Press), 24-33.

Gauchat, L. 1905. "L'unité phonétique dans le patois d'une commune." *Festschrift Heinrich Morf* (Halle, *Romanische Sprachen und Literaturen*), 175-232.

Gauthiot, R. 1912. "Du nombre duel." *Festschrift Vilhelm Thomsen* (Leipzig: Harrassowitz), 127-133.

Glasrud, Clarence A. 1963. *Hjalmar Hiorth Boyesen*. Northfield, Minn.: Norwegian-American Historical Association.

Glazer, Nathan and Daniel Moynihan. 1963a. *Beyond the Melting Pot*. Cambridge, Mass.: M.I.T. Press and Harvard University Press.

—. 1963b. "Why Ethnicity?" *Commentary* 58. 33-39.

—. eds. 1975. *Ethnicity: Theory and Experience*. Cambridge, Mass.: Harvard University Press.

Green, Julian. 1941. "An Experiment in English." *Harper's Magazine* 183. 397-405.

Greenberg, Joseph H. 1966. "Language Universals." *Current Trends in Linguistics* (The Hague: Mouton) 3. 73-113.

Grosjean, François. 1982. *Life with Two Languages: An Introduction to Bilingualism*. Cambridge, Mass.: Harvard University Press.

Guðmundsson, Helgi. 1972. *The Pronominal Dual in Icelandic*. Reykjavík: Institute of Nordic Linguistics.

Gumperz, John. 1962. "Types of Linguistic Communities." *Anthropological Linguistics* 4. 1. 28-40. [Repr. in his *Language in Social Groups*, ed. A. Dil, Stanford, Cal.: Stanford University, 1962, pp. 97-113].

—. 1964. "Linguistic and Social Interaction in Two Communities." *American Anthropologist* 66. 6. 2. 137-153.

—. 1965. "Linguistic Repertoires, Grammars, and Second Language Instruction." *Georgetown University Monograph Series 18* (Washington, D.C.) 81-90.

—. 1967. "On the Linguistic Markers of Bilingual Communication." *Journal of Social Issues* 23. 48-57.

Hagström, Björn. 1977. "'Hvi hevur nekarin fepur?': Något om form, uttal och stavning av danska lånord i färöiskan." *Fróðskaparrit* 25. 26-56.

Hall, Robert A. 1952. "Bilingualism and Applied Linguistics." *Zeitschrift für Phonetik und allgemeine Sprachwissenschaft* 6. 13-20.

Hammerich, L.L. 1959. "Wenn der Dualis lebendig ist–." *Die Sprache* 5. 16-26.

Hansegård, Nils Erik. 1967. "Recent Finnish Loanwords in Jukkasjärvi Lappish." *Acta Universitatis Upsaliensis* (Studia Uralica et Altaica 3).

—. 1968. *Tvåspråkighet eller halvspråkighet?* Stockholm: Aldus/Bonniers [4. ed. 1974].

Hasselmo, Nils. 1974. *Amerikasvenska: En bok om språkutvecklingen i Svensk-Amerika*. Stockholm: Esselte Studium.

Haugen, Einar. 1931. "Norwegians at the Indian Forts on the Missouri River During the Seventies." *Norwegian-American Studies and Records* 6. 89-121.

—. 1939. *Norsk i Amerika*. Oslo: Cappelen. [2. ed. 1975. Oslo: Cappelen].

—. 1949. "A Norwegian-American Pioneer Ballad." *Norwegian-American Studies and Records* 15. 1-19.

—. 1953a. *The Norwegian Language in America: A Study in Bilingual Behavior*. 2 vols. Philadelphia: Univ. of Pennsylvania Press/Oslo: The American Institute [Repr. 1969 Bloomington, Ind.: Indiana University Press].

—. 1953b. "Nordiske språkproblemer – en opinionsundersøkelse." *Nordisk Tidskrift* 29. 225-249.

—. 1956. *Bilingualism in the Americas: A Bibliography and Research Guide*. University, Ala.: American Dialect Society (PADS No. 26).

—. 1962. "Schizoglossia and the Linguistic Norm." *Georgetown University Monograph Series on Language and Linguistics* 15 (Washington, D.C.), 63-73.

—. 1966a. *Language Conflict and Language Planning: The Case of Modern Norwegian*. Cambridge, Mass.: Harvard University Press.

—. 1966b. "Linguistics and Language Planning." *Sociolinguistics*, ed. W. Bright (The Hague: Mouton), 50-71.

—. 1966c. "Semicommunication: The Language Gap in Scandinavia." *Sociological Inquiry* 36. 280-297. [Repr. in Haugen 1972, 215-236].

—. 1968. "The Scandinavian Languages as Cultural Artifacts." *Language Problems of Developing Nations*, ed. J. Fishman, C. Ferguson, J. Das Gupta (New York: Wiley), 267-284.

—. 1971. "Instrumentalism in Language Planning." *Can Language Be Planned?*, ed. J. Rubin and B. Jernudd (Honolulu: University Press of Hawaii), 281-289.

—. 1972a. *The Ecology of Language*, ed. A.S. Dil. Stanford, Cal.: Stanford University Press.

—. 1972b. "The Stigmata of Bilingualism." In Haugen 1972a, 307-324.

—. 1973a. "Bilingualism, Language Contact, and Immigrant Languages in the United States: A Research Report 1956-1970." *Current Trends in Linguistics 10*, ed. T. Sebeok (The Hague: Mouton), 505-591.

—. 1973b. "The Curse of Babel." *Language as a Human Problem*, ed. M. Bloomfield and E. Haugen (New York: Norton), 33-43.

—. 1976a. *The Scandinavian Languages: An Introduction to Their History*. London: Faber and Faber/Cambridge, Mass. Harvard Univ. Press.

—. 1976b. "A Case of Grass-roots Historiography: Opdalslaget and its Yearbooks." *Norwegian Influence on the Upper Midwest*, ed. Harald S. Næss (Duluth: University of Minnesota-Duluth), 42-49.

—. 1978. "Bilingualism in Retrospect — a Personal View. *Georgetown University Round Table 1978*, ed. James E. Alatis, 35-41.

—. 1979. *Ibsen's Drama: Author to Audience*. Minneapolis: University of Minnesota Press.

—. 1980. "On the Making of a Linguist." *First Person Singular*, ed. Boyd H. Davis and Raymond O'Cain (Amsterdam: Benjamins).

—. 1982. *Oppdalsmålet: Innføring i et sørtrøndsk fjellbygdmål*. Oslo: Tanum-Norli.

—. 1983. "The Rationale of Language Choice." *Proceedings of the 13th Intern. Congress of Linguists* (Tokyo), 317-328.

Haugen, Eva L. 1974. "The Story of Peder Anderson." *Norwegian-American Studies* 26. 31-47.

Haugen, Eva L. and Ingrid Semmingsen. 1973. "Peder Anderson of Bergen and Lowell: Artist and Ambassador of Culture." *Americana Norvegica* (Oslo: Universitetsforlaget) 4. 1-29.

Heath, Shirley Brice. 1972. *Telling Tongues: Language Policy in Mexico, Colony to Nation*. New York: Teachers College Press (Columbia University).

—. 1974. "Colonial Language Status Achievement: Mexico, Peru, and the United States." Paper, 8. World Congress of Sociology, Toronto, Canada, August 1974.

Hedblom, Folke. 1975. "Svenska dialekter i Amerika." *K. Humanistiska Vetenskapssamfundet i Uppsala årsbok 1973*, 4. 34-62.

Hellevik, Alf. 1963. *Lånord-problemet. To foredrag i Norsk Språknemnd med eit tillegg*. Oslo: Norsk Språknemnd (Småskrifter 2).

Herman, Simon R. 1961. "Explorations in the Social Psychology of Language Choice." *Human Relations* 14. 149-164. [Repr. Fishman, *Readings*, 1968, 492-511].

Hertzler, Joyce O. 1965. *A Sociology of Language*. New York: Random House.

Hickerson, H., G.D. Turner, and Nancy P. Hickerson. 1952. "Testing Procedures for Estimating Tranfer of Information among Iroquois Dialects and Languages." *Intern. Journ. of American Linguistics* 18. 1-8

Hockett, Charles A. 1958. *A Course in Modern Linguistics*. New York: MacMillan.

Hoijer, Harry, ed. 1954. *Language in Culture*. Chicago: University of Chicago Press.

Hollingshead, August B. 1950. "Cultural Factors in the Selection of Marriage Mates." *American Sociological Review* 15. 619-627.

Homans, George. 1958. "Social Behavior as Exchange." *Amer. Journal of Sociology* 63, 596-606.

Howard, John N. 1971-1975. "From the Editor." *Applied Optics* (Aug. 71, Dec. 71, Feb. 72, Apr. 72, Je 72, Oct. 72, May 74, Jan. 75).

Humboldt, Wilhelm von. 1963 [1827]. "Uber den Dualis." *Werke in fünf Banden* III (Stuttgart: Cotta).

Hymes, Dell. 1962. "The Ethnography of Speaking." *Anthropology and Human Behavior*, eds. T. Gladwin and W.S. Sturtevant (Washington, D.C.), 13-63. [Repr. in Fishman 1968, 99-138].

—. ed. 1964. *Language in Culture and Society: A Reader in Linguistics and Anthropology*. New York: Harper and Row.

Hymes, Dell and William E. Bittle, eds. 1967. *Studies in South-western Ethnolinguistics*. The Hague: Mouton.

Ingers, Ingemar. 1974. "Uniformiteten och Skånes folkmål." *Ale: Historisk tidskrift för Skåneland*, Nr. 3, 31-43.

Isaacs, Harold. "Basic Group Identity: The Idols of the Tribe." In Glazer and Moynihan 1975, 29-83.

Jaakkola, Magdalena. 1971. "Språk och sociala möjligheter i svenska Tornedalen," *Studier kring gränsen i Tornedalen*, ed. E. Haavio-Mannila and K. Suolinna (Stockholm: Nordiska Rådet), 119-128.

Jakobson, Roman. 1964. "Zur Struktur des russischen Verbums." *A Prague School Reader in Linguistics*, ed. J. Vachek. (Bloomington, Ind.: Indiana Univ. Press), 347-359.

Jensen, Anker. 1898. "Sproglige forhold i Åby sogn, Århus amt." *Dania* 5. 213-238.

Jernudd, Björn and J. Das Gupta. 1971. "Towards a Theory of Language Planning." *Can Language be Planned?*, ed. J. Rubin and B. Jernudd, 217-252. [Repr. Fishman 1972 *Advances*, pp. 476-510].

Jespersen, Otto. 1902. "Engelsk og nordisk." *Nordisk Tidskrift för Vetenskap, Konst och Industri* 2. 500-544.

—. 1906/07. "Mands Sprog og Kvindes Tale." *Gads Danske Magasin*, 581-592. [Repr. in *Language* (London 1922), 237-254].

—. 1924. *The Philosophy of Grammar*. London: Allen and Unwin.

Johnson, Walter. 1942. "American Loanwords in American Swedish." *Scandinavian Studies* (*Flom Festskrift*), ed. H. Larsen and C.A. Williams (Urbana, Ill.: Univ. of Illinois Press), 79-91.

—. 1971. "The Recording of American Swedish." *Americana Norvegica* 3.64-73 (Oslo).

Jonsson, Bengt R. 1974. "Visor i emigrationens spår." *Från Kulturdagarna i Bonäs bygdegård den 25-27 juni 1973* (Uppsala).

Karam, Francis X. 1974. "Toward a Definition of Language Planning." *Advances in Language Planning*, ed. J. Fishman (The Hague: Mouton), 103-124.

—. 1975. "Mutual Intelligibility and Sociolinguistic Surveys." Conference on the Methodology of Sociolinguistic Surveys, Montreal, May 19-21, 1975. Stenciled.

Karttunen, Frances and Kate Moore. 1974. "Finnish in America: Two Kinds of Finglish." Paper, Linguistic Society of America, December, 1974.

Kelly, L.G. ed. 1969. *Description and Measurement of Bilingualism: an International Seminar, University of Moncton, June 6-14, 1967.* Toronto: University of Toronto Press.

Kirk, James. 1905. *The Norsk Nightingale: Being the Lyrics of a "Lumberyack."* New York: Dodd Mead and Co. [17th Printing 1929].

Kirk, Paul L. 1970. "Dialect Intelligibility Testing: The Mazatec Study." *Intern. Journal of Amer. Linguistics* 36. 205-211.

Kjær, Iver and M. Baumann-Larsen. 1973. "'Tings gik like that.'" *Danske Studier*, 108-118.

—. 1974. "'De messy ting.' Om kodeskift i danskamerikansk." *Festskrift til Kristian Hald*, ed. P. Andersen (Copenhagen: Akademisk Forlag), 421-430.

Kloss, Heinz. 1969. *Research Possibilities on Group Bilingualism: A Report.* Quebec: Intern. Center for Research on Bilingulaism.

—. 1978. *Die Entwicklung neuer germanischen Kultursprachen.* 2. rev. ed. Dusseldorf: Schwann. [1. ed. 1952].

Kobrick, Jeffrey W. 1972. "The Compelling Case for Bilingual Education." *Saturday Review*, April 29, 54-58.

Koch, G.H. von. 1910. *Emigranternas Land: Studier i amerikansk samhällslif.* Stockholm: Aktiebolaget Ljus.

Kolers, Paul A. 1968. "Bilingualism and Information Processing." *Scientific American* 218. 78-86.

Labov, William. 1965. "On the Mechanisms of Linguistic Change." *Georgetown University Monograph Series 18* (Washington, D.C.), 91-114.

—. 1966. *The Social Stratification of English in New York City.* Washington, D.C.: Center for Applied Linguistics.

—. 1969. "The Logic of Nonstandard English." *Georgetown Monographs in Languages and Linguistics* 22. 1-45.

—. 1970. "The Study of Language in its Social Context." *Studium Generale* 23. 30-87.

—. 1972. *Sociolinguistic Patterns.* Philadelphia: University of Pennsylvania Press.

Lakoff, Robin. 1973. "Language and Woman's Place." *Language in Society* 2. 45-79.

Lambert, Wallace, et al. 1960. "Evaluational Reactions to Spoken Languages." *Journ. of Abnormal and Social Psychology* 60. 44-51.

—. 1961. "Behavioral Evidence for Contrasting Forms .of Bilingualism." *Georgetown University Round Table* (Washington, D.C.: Georgetown University Press), 14. 73-79.

—. 1974. "A Canadian Experiment in the Development of Bilingual Competence." *Canadian Modern Language Review* 31. 108-116.

Lance, Donald. 1979. "Spanish-English Bilingualism in the American Southwest." *Sociolinguistic Studies in Language Contact: Methods and Cases,* ed. W.F. Mackey and J. Ornstein (The Hague: Mouton), 247-264.

Larsen, Amund B. and Gerhard Stoltz. 1912. *Bergens bymål.* Kristiania: Bymålslaget.

Leibowitz, Arnold H. 1973. "Language and the Law: the Exercise of Political Power through Official Designation of the Language." 1973. *Language and Politics,* ed. Wm. M. O'Barr and Jean F. O'Barr (The Hague: Mouton), 449-466.

Leopold, Werner F. 1939-1949. *Speech Development of a Bilingual Child.* 4 vols. Evanston, Ill.: Northwestern University Studies.

Levine, Lewis and Harr J. Crockett, Jr. "Speech Variation in a Piedmont Community: Postvocalic r." *Explorations in Sociolinguistics,* ed S. Lieberson (Bloomington, Ind.: Univ. Press), 76-98.

Lieberson, Stanley. 1969. "How can we Describe and Measure the Incidence and Distribution of Bilingualism?" Kelly, L. ed. 1969, 286-295.

Lieberson, Stanley, and Lynn K. Hansen. 1974. "National Development, Mother Tongue Diversity, and the Comparative Study of Nations." *American Sociological Review* 39. 523-554.

Lieberson, Stanley, and James F. O'Connor. 1975a. "Language Diversity in a Nation and in Regions." *Multilingual Political Systems: Problems and Solutions,* ed. by Jean-Guy Savard and Richard Vigneault (Quebec: Université Laval), 161-181.

Lieberson, Stanley, et al. 1975b. "The Course of Mother-Tongue Diversity in Nations." *American Journal of Sociology* 81. 34-61.

Lindmark, Sture. 1971. *Swedish America 1914-1932: Studies in Ethnicity with Emphasis on Illinois and Minnesota.* Uppsala: Studia Historica Upsaliensia 37.

Ljunggren, K.G, 1956. "Den nordiska språkvården och de nya orden." *Nordiske språkspørsmål 1956,* 16-27.

Lovoll, Odd S. 1975. *A Folk Epic: The Bygdelag in America.* Boston: Twayne (for the Norw.-Am. Hist. Assoc.).

Lowie, Robert H. 1945. "A Case of Bilingualism." *Word* 1. 249-259.

Mackey, William F. 1965. "Bilingual Interference: Its Analysis and Measurement." *Journal of Communication* 15. 239-249.

Maclay, Howard Stanley. 1958. "An Experimental Study of Language and Non-linguistic Behavior." *Southwestern Journal of Anthropology* 14. 220-229.

Macnamara, John. 1966. *Bilingualism and Primary Education: A Study of Irish Experience.* Edinburgh: University Press.

—. 1970. *Bilingualism and Thought.* Georgetown University Monograph Series on Languages and Linguistics 23 (Washington, D.C.).

Maurud, Øivind. 1976. *Nabospråksforståelse i Skandinavia.* Stockholm: Nordiska rådet (Nordisk utredningsserie 13).

McGuire, Carson. 1950. "Social Stratification and Mobility Patterns." *American Sociological Review* 15. 195-204.

Mjöberg, Jöran. 1960. "Nybyggarnas språk." *Svenska Dagbladet,* April 27.

Moberg, Vilhelm. 1949-1959. *Utvandrarna; Invandrarna; Nybyggarna; Sista*

Brevet till Sverige [Novels]. Stockholm: Bonniers.

Molde, Bertil, ed. 1976. *Fackspråk: en antologi.* Stockholm: Svenska språknämnden.

Molde, Bertil and Allan Karker, eds. 1983. *Språkene i Norden/Språken i Norden/Sprogene i Norden.* Nordisk språksekretariat.

Nadkarni, M.V. 1975. "Bilingualism and Syntactic Change in Konkani." *Language* 51. 672-683.

National Bureau of Standards. 1971. *Special Publication* 330. Washington, D.C. [Revised version 1977: *The International System of Units* (SI)].

Nelson, Helge. 1943. *The Swedes and the Swedish Settlements in North America.* 2 vols. Lund: Gleerup.

Nemser, William. 1969. "Approximative Systems of Foreign Language Learners." *The Yugoslav Serbo-Croation-English Contrastive Project, Studies B.1.* Zagreb: Institute of Linguistics.

Neustupný, Jiri. 1970. "Basic Types of Treatment of Language Problems." *Linguistic Communications* 1. 77-98 [Repr. in Fishman, ed. 1974, 37-48.]

—. 1978. *Post-Structural Approaches to Language: Language Theory in a Japanese Context.* Tokyo: Univ. of Tokyo Press.

Nordiskt språksekretariat. 1977. Oslo: Nordiska rådet och Nordiska Ministerrådet.

Norman, Hans. 1974. *Från Bergslagen till Nordamerika.* Uppsala: Studia Historica Upsaliensia 62.

Österberg, Tore. 1961. *Bilingualism and the First School Language.* Umeå (Diss. Univ. of Uppsala).

Oftedal, Magne. 1973. "Notes on Language and Sex." *Norwegian Journal of Linguistics* 27. 67-75.

Ohlsson, Stig Örjan. 1978-79. *Skånes språkliga försvenskning.* 2 vols. Lund: Lundastudier i nordisk språkvetenskap (Serie A, nr. 30, 31).

—. 1979. *Nordisk språkförståelse – igår, idag, imorgon.* Nordiska Ministerrådet 1979: 6.

Oksaar, Els. 1979. "Models of Competence in Bilingual Interaction." *Sociolinguistic Studies in Language Contact*, ed. W.F. Mackey and J. Ornstein (The Hague: Mouton), 99-113.

Olmsted, D.L. 1954. "Achumawi-Atsuwegi Non-Reciprocal Intelligibility." *Intern. Journ. of Amer. Linguistics* 20. 181-184.

Osgood, Charles E. 1954. *Psycholinguistics: A Survey of Theory and Research Problems.* Baltimore: Waverley Press. (Suppl. to *Journ. of Abnormal and Social Psych.*, vol. 49, No. 4, part 2).

Paradis, Michel, ed. 1978. *Aspects of Bilingualism.* Columbia, S.C.: Hornbeam Press.

Paulston, Christina Bratt. 1975. "Language Universals and Sociocultural Implications." *Studia Linguistica* 29. 1-15.

—. 1974. "Questions Concerning Bilingual Education." Paper, Interamerican Conference on Bilingual Education, Amer. Anthr. Assn., Mexico City, Nov. 22, 1974.

Pierce, Joe E. 1952. "Dialect Distance Testing in Algonquian." *Intern. Jour. of Amer. Linguistics* 18. 203-210.

Pike, Kenneth L. 1967. *Language in Relation to a Unified Theory of the Structure of Human Behavior.* 2. ed. The Hague: Mouton.

Qualey, Carlton C. 1938. *Norwegian Settlement in the United States.* Northfield, Minn.: Norwegian-American Historical Association.

Rafky, David M. 1970. "The Semantics of Negritude." *American Speech* 45. 30-45.

Ray, P.S. 1963. *Language Standardization: Studies in Prescriptive Linguistics.* The Hague: Mouton.

Read, Allen Walker. 1974. "What is 'Linguistic Imperialism'?" *Geolinguistics* 1. 5-10.

Rubin, Joan. 1968. "Language Education in Paraguay." *Language Problems of Developing Nations*, ed. J. Fishman, C. Ferguson, and J. Das Gupta (New York: Wiley), 477-488.

—. 1971. "Evaluation and Language Planning." *Can Language be Planned?*, ed. by J. Rubin and B. Jernudd (Honolulu: East-West Center and the Univ. of Hawaii), 217-252 [Repr. in Fishman, *Advances* 1974, 476-510].

Rubin, Joan and Björn Jernudd. 1977. *References for Students of Language Planning.* Honolulu: East-West Center.

Rūķe-Draviņa, Velta. 1967. *Mehrsprachigkeit im Vorschulalter.* Lund: Gleerup (Travaux de l'Institut de Phonétique de Lund, V).

Runblom, Harald and Hans Norman, eds. 1976. *From Sweden to America.* Minneapolis and Uppsala: Univ. of Minnesota Press and Univ. of Uppsala.

Ruong, Israel. 1969. *Samerna.* Stockholm: Aldus/Bonniers.

Sapir, Leonard. 1921. *Language: An Introduction to the Study of Speech.* New York: Harcourt Brace.

—. 1929. "The Status of Linguistics as a Science." *Language* 5. 207-214.

Saville, Muriel R. and Rudolph C. Troike. 1971. *A Handbook of Bilingual Education.* Washington, D.C. (TESOL).

Schermerhorn, R. A. 1964. "Toward a General Theory of Minority Groups." *Phylon* 25. 238-246.

Schmidt, W. 1926. *Die Sprachfamilien und Sprachenkreise der Erde.* Heidelberg: Winter.

Scotton, Carol Myers. 1972. *Choosing a Lingua Franca in an African Capital.* Edmonton/Champaign: Linguistic Research, Inc. (Sociolinguistic Series 2).

—. 1976. "Strategies of Neutrality: Language Choice in Uncertain Situations." *Language* 52. 919-941.

Shaffer, Douglas. 1975. "The Place of Code Switching in Linguistic Contact." Unprinted paper.

Shibutani, Tamotsu and Kian M. Kwan. 1965. *Ethnic Stratification.* New York: Macmillan.

Sigurd, Bengt, ed. 1977. *De nordiske språkenes framtid.* Oslo: Norsk språkråd (Skrifter 19).

Skaardal, Dorothy. 1974. *The Divided Heart.* Oslo: Universitetsforlaget.

Skard, Sigmund. 1980. *Classical Tradition in Norway.* Oslo: Universitetsforlaget.

Skarstedt, Ernst. 1890. *Svensk-Amerikanska Poeter i ord och bild.* Minneapolis, Minn.

162   *Blessings of Babel*

Skautrup, Peter. 1944-1970. *Det danske sprogs historie.* 5 vols. Copenhagen: Gyldendal.

Skutnabb-Kangas, Tove. 1981. *Tvåspråkighet.* Lund: Liber Läromedel.

Søndergård, Bent. 1978. "Tosprogethedsproblemer i det dansktyske grænseområde" (Åbenrå: Institut for grænseregionsforskning), 58-67.

—. 1980. "Sprogkontakt i den dansk-tyske grænseregion: Interferensproblematikken." *Fourth Intern. Conference of Nordic and General Linguistics* (Oslo), Abstracts 127.

Sokol, Louis, ed. 1975. *United States Metric Association Newsletter* (quarterly) 10(2). Boulder, Colo.

—. 1978. *Statement on the Spelling of Metre.* USMA Metric Practice Committee, U.S. Metric Association.

Sommerfelt, Alf. 1935. *Sproget som samfundsorgan.* Oslo: J.M. Stenersen (Universitetets Radioforedrag).

Språkvård: Redogörelser och studier utgivna till språkvårdsnämndens tioårsdag 1954. 1954. Stockholm: Svenska Bokförlaget. (Skrifter utgivna av Nämnden för svensk språkvård 11).

Stefansson, Vilhjalmur. 1903. "English Loan-nouns Used in the Icelandic Colony of North Dakota." *Dialect Notes* 2. 354-362.

Steinsholt, Anders. 1964. *Målbryting i Hedrum.* Oslo: Universitetsforlaget (Skrifter frå Norsk Målførearkiv 19).

Stene, Aasta. 1945. *English Loan-words in Modern Norwegian: A Study of Linguistic Borrowing in the Process.* London/Oslo: The Philological Society (Oxford Univ. Press/Tanum).

Stewart, William. 1964. "Urban Negro Speech." *Social Dialects and Language Learning,* ed. Roger Shuy (Champaign, Ill.: University of Illinois Press), 10-18.

—. 1968. "A Sociolinguistic Typology for Describing National Multilingualism." *Readings in the Sociology of Language,* ed. J. Fishman (The Hague: Mouton) 531-545.

Sutton, Geoffrey. 1979. "Cultural and Socio-economic Factors in the Formation of Foreign Language Education Policy in Sweden — with a Comparison with the Finnish Case." *Language Problems and Language Planning* 3. 9-24.

Svalestuen, Andres A. 1971. "Nordisk emigrasjon — en komparativ oversikt." *Emigrationen fra Norden indtil l. Verdenskrig.* Copenhagen: Rapporter til det Nordiske historikermøde i København 1971).

Swadesh, Morris. 1948. "Sociologic Notes on Obsolescent Languages." *Intern. Journ. of Amer. Linguistics* 14. 226-235.

Tauli, Valter. 1968. *Introduction to a Theory of Language Planning.* Uppsala: Acta Univ. Upsal. (Studia Philologiae Scandinavica 6).

Tegnér, Esaias. 1880. *Språkets makt över tanken.* [Repr. in his *Ur språkens värld* 1. 165-346 (Stockholm: Bonnier 1922)].

Tengström, Emil. 1973. *Latinet i Sverige.* Lund: Bonniers.

Teske, Raymond H.C., Jr. and Bardin H. Nelson. 1974. "Acculturation and Assimilation: A Clarification." *American Ethnologist* 1. 341-367.

Tesnière, Lucien. 1925. *Les formes du duel en slovène.* Paris: H. Champion.
Thibaut, John and Harold Kelley. 1959. *The Social Psychology of Groups.* New York: Wiley.
Thorne, Barrie and Nancy Henley, ed. 1975. *Sex and Language: Difference and Dominance.* Rowley, Mass.: Newbury House.
Tingbjörn, Gunnar. 1976. "Sportsspråket i spalterna – ett målrelaterat språk." *Språket i spalterna*, ed. Lars Alfvegren et al. (Lund: Studentlitteratur) 89-112 (Ord och stil 8).
Tylden, Per. 1944. *Me – vi, ein studie frå det gamalnorske og mellomnorske brevriket.* Oslo: Skrifter av det Norske Videnskapsakademi.
Ureland, P. Sture. 1971. "Report on Texas-Swedish Research." *Svenska Landsmål och Svenskt Folkliv* 295. 27-74.
–. 1975. "The Swedish Language in America." *Svenska Landsmål och Svenskt Folkliv* 300. 83-105. (Review of Hasselmo 1974).
Valdes-Fallís, Guadalupe. 1976. "Social Interaction and Code-Switching Patterns." *Bilingualism in the Bicentennial and Beyond*, ed. Keller et al. (New York: Bilingual Press), 53-85.
Valette, Rebecca M. 1964. "Some Reflections of Second-Language Learning in Children." *Language Learning* 14. 91-98.
Vildomec, V. 1963. *Multilingualism.* Leyden: Sythoff.
Voegelin, Carl F. and Zellig Harris. 1950. "Methods for Determining Intelligibility among Dialects of Natural Languages." *Proceedings, American Philssophical Society* 95. 322-329.
Voegelin, Carl F. 1960. "Casual and Non-Casual Utterances Within Unified Structure." *Style in Language*, ed. T. Sebeok (Cambridge, Mass.: M.I.T. Press), 57-68.
Vogt, Hans. 1970. "De små språksamfunn: Noen betraktninger." *The Nordic Languages and Modern Linguistics*, ed. H. Benediktsson (Reykjavík: Vísindafélag), 306-310.
Wackernagel, J. 1950-1957. *Vorlesungen über Syntax.* 2 vols. Basel: Philologisches Seminar.
Wande, Erling. 1977. "Hansegård är ensidig." *Invandrare och Minoriteter*, 41-51.
Watkins, Calvert. 1969. *Indogermanische Grammatik 3, Formenlehre.* Heidelberg: Winter.
Weinreich, Uriel. 1953. *Languages in Contact: Findings and Problems.* New York: Linguistic Circle of New York.
–. 1955. Review of Hoijer 1954. *Word* 11. 426-430.
Weinreich, Uriel, William Labov, and George Herzog. 1968. "Empirical Foundations for a Theory of Language Change." *Directions for Historical Linguistics*, ed. W. P. Lehmann and Y. Malkiel (Austin, Texas), 95-195.
Weiss, Andreas von. 1959. *Hauptprobleme der Zweisprachigkeit: Eine Untersuchung auf Grund deutsch/estnischen Materials.* Heidelberg: Winter.
Wennås, Olof. 1966. *Striden om latinväldet: Idéer och intressen i svensk skolpolitik under 1800-talet.* Stockholm: Almqvist och Wiksell (Skrifter utg. av Statsvet. Föreningen i Uppsala, 45).

Whiteley, Wilfred. 1969. *Swahili: The Rise of a National Language*. London: Methuen.

Whorf, Benjamin. 1956. *Language, Thought, and Reality*, ed. John B. Carroll. New York, London: M.I.T. Press/Wiley.

Wieczerkowski, Wilhelm. 1963. *Bilinguismus im frühen Schulalter*. Helsinki: Soc. Sci. Fennica, Commentationes Humanarum Litterarum XXXII. 2.

Index

MULTILINGUA

Journal of Cross-Cultural and Interlanguage Communication

Call for Papers

As from volume 6, 1987, the editorial programme of MULTILINGUA has been redirected towards presenting a forum for the discussion of research on social and cultural problems of communication in multilingual, multicultural settings.

Emphasis will be placed on constraints imposed upon the choice of linguistic system by the type of social activity in which the verbal interaction takes place.

Papers on the following range of topics are invited:
- cross-cultural differences in linguistic politeness phenomena
- strategies for the organization of verbal interaction
- variety within what is traditionally regarded as one culture
- conversational styles and the linguistic description of non-standard, oral varieties of language
- communication breakdown in interethnic, multicultural interaction
- formal and functional differences between standard and non-standard language
- cross-cultural problems in translation

Contributions will be considered in the form of empirical, observational studies, theoretical studies, theoretical discussions, presentation of research, short notes, reactions/replies to recent articles, review articles and letters to the editor. A copy of the style sheet will be sent on request.

Contributors should send three copies of the manuscript (two copies in the case of reviews) and an abstract of the article (not more than 150 words) to the following address:

Professor Richard Watts
The Editor, MULTILINGUA
Englisches Seminar
Gesellschaftsstrasse 6
CH – 3012 BERN
SWITZERLAND

mouton de gruyter

Berlin · New York · Amsterdam

Joshua A. Fishman, Andrée Tabouret-Keller,
Michael Clyne, Bh. Krishnamurti and
M. Abdulaziz (Eds.)

The Fergusonian Impact

In Honor of Charles A. Ferguson on the
Occasion of his 65th Birthday, 2 Volumes

1986. 14,8 x 22,8 cm. Vol. 1: XII, 598 pages; Vol. 2: XII, 545 pages.
Hardback volumes 1 and 2: DM 435,–; approx. US $229.00
ISBN 3 11 010487 3
(Contributions to the Sociology of Language 42)

The two-volume **Fergusonian Impact** contains 81 articles, bringing
together 85 anthropologists, linguists, psycholinguists and sociolinguists
from literally all corners of the world. This vast undertaking reflects the
truly international scope of Professor Ferguson's influence.

Volume 1: From Phonology to Society
I. Linguistics, child language and language and the child – II. Arabic
and languages of Africa – III. Applied linguistics.

Volume 2: Sociolinguistics and the Sociology of Language
IV. Microsociolinguistics: acts, actors and events – V. Sociolinguistic
situation and bilingual variation – VI. Language planning: corpus and
status – VII. Diglossia: particular cases and general reexamination –
VIII. Language contact, spread, maintenance and death – IX. Charles A.
Ferguson bibliography, 1945–1985.

A Special Issue of **The International Journal of the Sociology
of Language** (62, 1986) complements **The Fergusonian Impact** with
articles by colleagues, admirers and former students of Professor
Ferguson, bringing the year of the "Fergiefest" to a conclusion.
(160 pages; DM 54,– or US $22.00 plus postage.)

Prices are subject to change without notice

mouton de gruyter

Berlin · New York · Amsterdam